Puzzle It!
Pre-Algebra Riddles

by Jay Waggoner

IncentivePublications

BY WORLD BOOK
a Scott Fetzer company

*Thanks to Megan Skerchock
for the drawing of the rabbit
in Puzzle 49.*

*Illustrated by Kathleen Bullock
Cover by Angela Stiff
Edited by Marjorie Frank*

Print Edition ISBN 978-0-86530-518-2
E-book Edition ISBN 978-1-62950-365-3 (PDF)

World Book, Inc.
180 North LaSalle Street
Suite 900
Chicago, Illinois 60601
U.S.A.

For information about World Book and Incentive Publications products, call **1-800-967-5325**, or visit our websites at **www.worldbook.com** and **www.incentivepublications.com.**

Printed in the United States of America by Integrated Books International, Dulles, Virginia

CONTENTS

WELCOME

TO THE FUN OF PRE-ALGEBRA RIDDLES

Everybody loves a puzzle! A puzzle is like an unsolved mystery, teasing you to be the one who unravels it. There are few things that match the feeling of satisfaction you experience when, after thinking long and hard about a puzzle, the solution suddenly materializes—clear as crystal. It is a truly magical moment, one of the wonders of the human brain.

Here's some more magic: When students wrestle with a puzzle, classroom learning is energized. Who can walk away from the invitation to tackle a puzzle? It's just too much fun to try to figure it out. Even the most reluctant students seem to wake up and be drawn into the solution process. But puzzles are much more than fun. They give the brain a workout and nurture problem-solving skills.

Every classroom and home should offer many puzzle-solving opportunities. The National Council of Teachers of Mathematics identifies problem solving as "the cornerstone of school mathematics." The critical-thinking and problem-solving skills that are honed while solving puzzles are basic. They apply to every facet and subject area. In solving puzzles, students make use of such thinking skills as logic, analysis, synthesis, sequencing, creativity, induction, and deduction—and they often must use several of these simultaneously. To solve puzzles, students must observe, ask questions, consider strategies, try different approaches, visualize different possibilities, and figure out why one thing works and another does not. Because of the highly visual and motor-skill components to puzzle solving, puzzles are adaptable to many learning styles and abilities. Often a student can "see" a concept or process in a puzzle, when it was hard to catch it in another form.

Puzzles must be a part of every serious curriculum. The puzzles in the **Puzzle It!** series challenge students to analyze information, apply previously-learned material, and stretch their critical-thinking skills.

ABOUT THE PUZZLES IN THIS BOOK

All of these puzzles sharpen skills related to using pre-algebra requirements. Students must use the algebraic concepts and processes at a level prerequisite to Algebra I in order to solve the puzzles. They will read, write, simplify, and evaluate expressions; factor expressions; use formulas, ratios, percents, and rates; solve equations of many kinds; graph points, linear equations, and inequalities; calculate with exponents; and use many other skills.

The puzzles have many uses within a classroom. A puzzle can warm up a student's brain at the beginning of a class period, or top off a class with a great mental exercise. A puzzle can inspire or introduce a lesson on a particular skill, motivate practice of a concept, assess how well a student "gets" a specific process, or solidify an idea the student has learned. However you use the puzzles, they will strengthen pre-algebra skills and sharpen minds at the same time.

How To Use The Puzzles

- Look over each puzzle carefully. Read the instructions at least twice.

- Consider the puzzle thoughtfully. Make sure the purpose of the puzzle is clear to you.

- Evaluate what it is you must figure out or find.

- Note that many of these math puzzles have riddles, jokes, or word puzzles as a part of the page. This means that you are asked to solve some math problems AND you are also asked to use a code to translate math solutions into letters or words.

- Think about the strategy you will use to solve the puzzle. Sometimes you can use more than one.

- If you need to, refresh the pre-algebra skill that is required to do the puzzle. For instance, you may need to brush up on operations with exponents or review how to graph inequalities.

- Take one puzzle at a time. A puzzle will grab you and won't let go until you figure it out. Stay with it until you reach a solution.

- Try not to look at the answers too quickly. Ask someone else for a hint or an idea if you need help.

- You can tackle a puzzle alone, or share a puzzle with someone else and tackle it together. Share ideas, discuss, argue, check each other's math—until you arrive at a solution.

- When you find a solution, discuss it with someone else. Explain the steps and strategies you used to reach your answer. Compare your solution and methods with someone else's.

About The Solutions . . .

The answer key gives solutions for all of the puzzles. In some cases, however, there may be more than one solution that makes sense. Give yourself or your students credit for any solution that can be explained and justified.

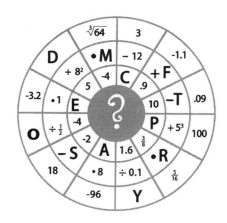

CAN YOU TALK TEXT?

Sam has sent a text message to let Pam know about something urgent. She has responded. To complete the conversation, solve the problem found in each sentence. Then place the letter (found after the sentence) in the blank above the number that matches your problem solution.

1. On New Year's Eve, 2007, and the next day, $-63 + 100$ billion text messages were sent in the U. S. **(G)**

2. There are $-3.7 + 7.0$ billion cell phones in the world. **(U)**

3. In the U.S., $2(-5)^2\%$ of kids under 18 have cell phones. **(B)**

4. In 2006, ring tone sales exceeded $(-13 + 18)$ billion dollars. **(S)**

5. $(-15)(-20)$ million cell phones are being used in the U.S. **(N)**

6. The average American owns $-3 - (-6)$ expired cell phones. **(D)**

7. $(-5)(7)(-2)\%$ of Americans do not know that they can recycle old phones. **(S)**

8. $4 - (-3)\%$ of Americans threw away old cell phones. **(T)**

9. 500,000,000 cell phones weighing $(-\frac{1}{4})(-10)^3$ tons are stockpiled and awaiting disposal. **(K)**

10. $-32 + (-28) + 120\%$ of the radiation emitted by a cell phone will be absorbed by the user's head. **(W)**

11. $(-2 \cdot 3)^2\%$ of cell phone users report having been shocked occasionally with their monthly bills. **(T)**

12. $(-10)(-4.6)\%$ of people interviewed said they "can't live without their cell phone." **(T)**

3	36	70	7	5

300	60

3.3	37	46	50	250

Bonus

What are they saying? Translate the text messages.

Sam: _____

Pam: _____

WHAT ARE THE POWERS OF LATIN?

If you know about powers of numbers, you can break the code to translate these Latin phrases. Match each number in the puzzle with an exponential Roman numeral (created especially for this riddle) of the same value. (You will find the special numerals in the KEY.) Then find the code letter next to that Roman numeral and write it in the blank.

KEY

X^{II} = A
II^{III} = B
III^{II} = C
$V \cdot X^{II}$ = D
V^{I} = E
IV^{II} = F
$X^{I} \cdot III^{II}$ = G
X^{I} = H
II^{V} = I
XI^{II} = K
V^{III} = L
II^{II} = M
VII^{II} = N
V^{II} = O
$V^{III} \cdot II$ = P
XXX^{II} = R
X^{III} = S
$II \cdot V^{II}$ = T
IX^{II} = U
$II^{II} \cdot V$ = V
$III^{II} \cdot II^{III}$ = W
XV^{II} = Y

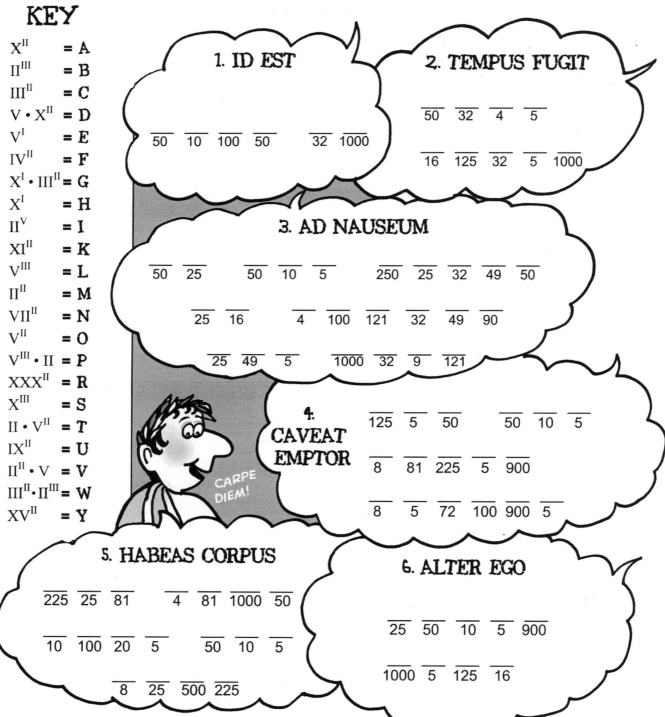

1. ID EST

___ ___ ___ ___ ___ ___
50 10 100 50   32 1000

2. TEMPUS FUGIT

___ ___ ___ ___
50 32 4   5

___ ___ ___ ___ ___
16 125 32 5 1000

3. AD NAUSEUM

___ ___ ___ ___ ___ ___ ___ ___ ___ ___
50 25   50 10 5   250 25 32 49 50

___ ___ ___ ___ ___ ___ ___
25 16   4   100 121 32 49 90

___ ___ ___ ___ ___ ___ ___
25 49 5   1000 32 9 121

4. CAVEAT EMPTOR

___ ___ ___ ___ ___ ___
125 5   50   50 10 5

___ ___ ___ ___ ___
8   81 225 5   900

___ ___ ___ ___ ___ ___
8   5   72 100 900 5

5. HABEAS CORPUS

___ ___ ___ ___ ___ ___ ___
225 25 81   4   81 1000 50

___ ___ ___ ___ ___ ___ ___
10 100 20 5   50 10 5

___ ___ ___ ___
8   25 500 225

6. ALTER EGO

___ ___ ___ ___ ___
25 50 10 5   900

___ ___ ___ ___
1000 5 125 16

CARPE DIEM!

HOW DOES SOMEONE LEARN TO SPEAK MATH?

Answer this riddle-question by matching the expressions in words to the same expressions in numbers and symbols. Draw a straight line to connect matching expressions. The line will pass through a letter and a number. Put the letter above that number every place it appears in the riddle below.

three less than twice a number ●

five more than a number ●

Five is greater than a number. ●

twice the sum of five and
another number ●

nine less than a number ●

Nine is less than a number. ●

Five is less than the square of
another number. ●

the difference between the square of
five and the square of another number ●

Five is the sum of a number and two. ●

three plus an unknown number ●

a number increased by eight ●

Six is greater than a number. ●

Fourteen is two more than a number. ●

a number diminished by ten ●

The sum of a number and three
is eleven. ●

D (5) **Y** (1) (2) **M** (7) (9) **G** **C** **E** (6) **A** (14) (15) **H** (13) **I** **N** (12) **L** **S** **R** (8) (11) (3) (10) (4) **T** **O**

● $5 > x$

● $5^2 - x^2$

● $14 = x + 2$

● $x + 5$

● $9 < x$

● $x + 3 = 11$

● $x + 3$

● $5 = x + 2$

● $3 + 2x$

● $2x - 3$

● $3 + x$

● $2(5 + x)$

● $6 > x$

● $x - 9$

● $x - 10$

● $2 + 5x$

● $5 < x^2$

● $x + 8$

● $x^2 - 5$

To speak math, you'll need . . .

— —   — — — — — —   — — —   — — — —
1 12   7 12 9 15 13 6 11   4 10   14 1 4 11

— — — — — — — — — !
5 13 3 4 13 10 12 1 8 2

Name_____

IS IT PIE OR PI THAT PUZZLES CHEF PIERRE?

Chef Pierre is a great cook, but he's not great at math. Tonight he must prepare chocolate silk pie for 24 guests. Alas! His only recipe serves eight! Help him out with the pi and pie problems. The pie below holds the missing measurements. Put the right one into each blank in the recipe.

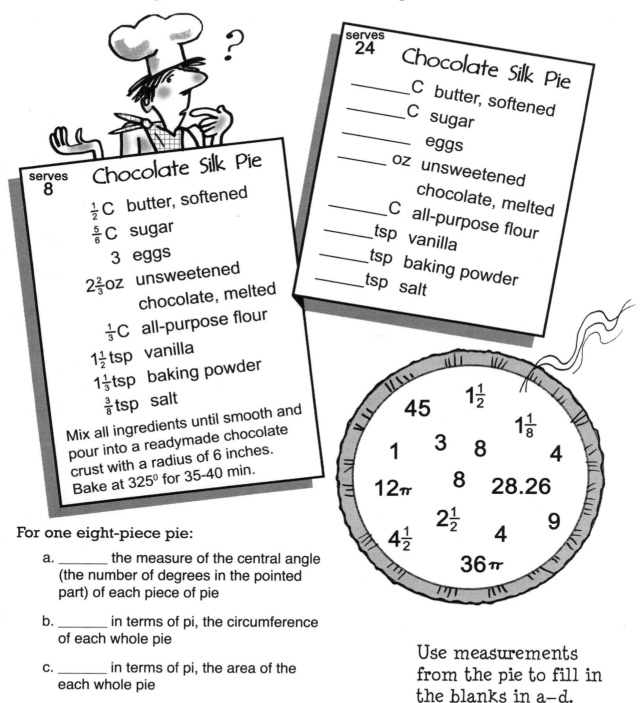

serves 24 — Chocolate Silk Pie

_____ C butter, softened

_____ C sugar

_____ eggs

_____ oz unsweetened chocolate, melted

_____ C all-purpose flour

_____ tsp vanilla

_____ tsp baking powder

_____ tsp salt

serves 8 — Chocolate Silk Pie

$\frac{1}{2}$ C butter, softened

$\frac{5}{6}$ C sugar

3 eggs

$2\frac{2}{3}$ oz unsweetened chocolate, melted

$\frac{1}{3}$ C all-purpose flour

$1\frac{1}{2}$ tsp vanilla

$1\frac{1}{3}$ tsp baking powder

$\frac{3}{8}$ tsp salt

Mix all ingredients until smooth and pour into a readymade chocolate crust with a radius of 6 inches. Bake at 325° for 35-40 min.

Numbers in pie: 45 $1\frac{1}{2}$ $1\frac{1}{8}$ 1 3 8 4 12π 8 28.26 $2\frac{1}{2}$ 9 $4\frac{1}{2}$ 4 36π

For one eight-piece pie:

a. _____ the measure of the central angle (the number of degrees in the pointed part) of each piece of pie

b. _____ in terms of pi, the circumference of each whole pie

c. _____ in terms of pi, the area of the each whole pie

d. _____ the volume of each person's piece of pie in cubic inches if the volume of each pie is about 72 π cubic inches

Use measurements from the pie to fill in the blanks in a–d.

Use 3.14 as value of π.

Name_____

WHEN IS THE PYTHAGOREAN THEOREM NOT "RIGHT"?

Those old Greeks really knew their mathematics. Study these flags waved by fans at some of the old Olympic Games. Find the missing measurements for each flag. Place the letter connected to the measurement into the puzzle space above that measurement.

At the bottom of the page, there is a puzzle to finish. It holds a clever answer to the riddle-question in the title.

1. Side A = _____
   S = the area of
   triangle 1 = _____

2. Side N = _____
   T = the area pf
   triangle 2 = _____

3. Side W = _____
   R = the perimeter of
   triangle 3 = _____

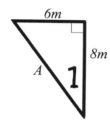

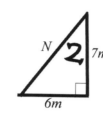

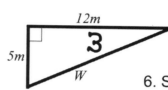

6. Side L = _____
   E = the perimeter of
   triangle 6 = _____

5. Side O = _____
   H = the area of
   triangle 5 = _____

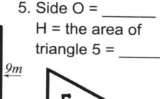

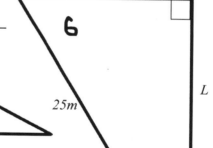

4. Side G = _____
   I = the perimeter of
   triangle 4 = _____

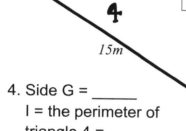

The Pythagorean Theorem works for:

___ ___ ___ ___ ___
30m 36m 12m 60m2 21m²

___ ___ ___ ___ ___ ___ ___ ___
21m² 30m 36m 10m √85m 12m 20m 60m 24m²

It does not work for:

___ ___ ___ ___ ___
13m 30m 17m √85m 12m

___ ___ ___ ___ ___ ___ ___ ___
21m² 30m 36m 10m √85m 12m 20m 60m 24m²

Name_____

Puzzle It! Pre-Algebra Riddles   11   ©Incentive Publications, Inc., Nashville, TN.

WHO'S WHO IN THIS TALENTED TRIO?

A fraction, a decimal, and a percent—they team up to make a trio with unique talents. Each one can name the same value. Solve the equation on each puzzle piece to get a decimal or percent answer. Then **convert the solution into a fraction** and use it to help solve the riddle below. Write the letter from the puzzle piece into the space above the matching fraction.

A ___ % of 80 = 16

E 36 = ___ % of 60

H ___ % of 5 = 2½

C 21 = ___ % of 30

N 20 x .005 = ___

I ? = .082 + .218

N 128 = ___ % of 160

F ___ % OF 36 = 27

W 2200 is ___ % of 2000

O 2.6 - 2.47 = ?

T ___ % of 48 = 12

R 3 = ___ % of 24

A ___ % of 72 = 27

S .1113 + .2887

I 42 = ___ % of 35

T 80 = ___ % of 2000

Riddle

When is a percent not a decimal?

$$\frac{11}{10} \quad \frac{1}{2} \quad \frac{3}{5} \quad \frac{1}{10} \qquad \frac{6}{5} \quad \frac{1}{4} \quad \frac{2}{5} \qquad \frac{1}{5} \qquad \frac{3}{4} \quad \frac{1}{8} \quad \frac{3}{8} \quad \frac{7}{10} \quad \frac{1}{25} \quad \frac{3}{10} \quad \frac{13}{100} \quad \frac{4}{5}$$

Name_____

WHICH ALPHABET IS IN MY SOUP?

This alphabet soup contains information about many different languages. Each letter holds an amount equal to the value of an expression below. Evaluate each expression and find the letter in the soup with that value. COLOR the letter. When you are finished with 1–12, follow the directions at the bottom of the page to find the alphabet named in the soup.

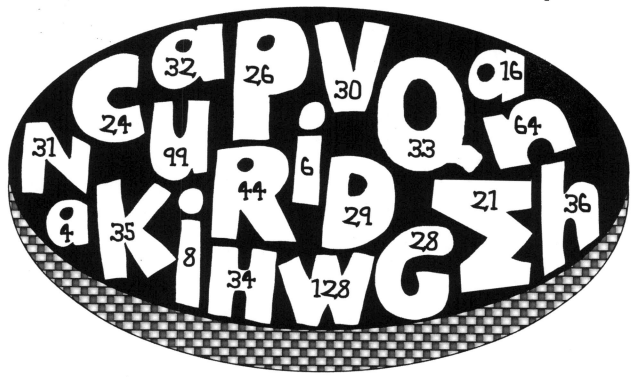

_____ 1. There are $2^4 + 2^3$ letters in the Greek alphabet.

_____ 2. The Japanese language has $2^6 + 2^5 + 2^1 + 2^0$ different sounds.

_____ 3. Both the French and the English languages have $2^4 + 2^3 + 2^1$ letters.

_____ 4. The Russian alphabet has $(2^2)(2^3) + 2^0$ letters.

_____ 5. To find the number of letters in the Spanish alphabet, evaluate: $2^5 - 2^1$.

_____ 6. There are $(2^{10} \div 2^5) - 2^1 - 2^0$ letters in the German alphabet.

_____ 7. If you write in Italian, you'll have $2^4 + 2^2 + 2^0$ letters available.

_____ 8. The Magyar and Hungarian alphabets both have $(2^2)(2^4) - 5(2^2)$ letters.

_____ 9. The Icelandic Alphabet has $(2^9 \div 2^4) + 2^1$ letters.

_____10. $(2^2)(2^3) + 2^0 + 2^1$ letter pairs make up the Latvian alphabet.

_____11. There are $2^{11} \div 2^6 - 2^0$ letters in the Macedonian alphabet.

_____12. The Thai alphabet has a lot of vowels: $(2^9 \div 2^4) - 2^2$, to be exact!

Bonus What language has only $(2^8 \div 2^4) + 2^1$ letter-sounds in its alphabet?

Unscramble the UNCOLORED LETTERS in the soup to find out.

Name_____

Puzzle 8

DOES THE CLUE FIT THE PUZZLE?

The crossword puzzle looks finished, but it seems that some of the clues are mixed up. Check each clue to see if it matches. If it does not, re-number the clue to show which word it DOES match.

ACROSS

____ 2. the equation whose graph is a straight line

____ 8. a number that, when multiplied with another number, yields a product of 1

____ 9. the elements in an equation

____ 11. a special ratio such as distance per time

____ 13. to find the value of an expression

____ 14. a number sentence showing two groups of numerals that stand for different amounts

____ 15. two perpendicular number lines that intersect at zero in a coordinate plane

____ 17. 1.5×10^5 is an example of _____ notation

____ 18. a number that can be written as the quotient of two numbers

____ 19. $2 + 3 + 4 = 4 + 2 + 3$ shows the commutative _____ for addition

____ 20. a number that yields a given product when multiplied by itself

DOWN

____ 1. a value that is the same distance from zero as a given number on the other side of zero from

____ 3. value shown in distance of a number from zero on a number line

____ 4. the number in the expression 4x

____ 5. one of the set of numbers greater than and less than zero

____ 7. a symbol meaning "the root of"

____ 10. a terminating decimal does not _____

____ 12. any number that is a positive number, a negative number, or zero

____ 16. the product of a number multiplied by itself once

Name_____

WHERE MIGHT YOU GO TO "STAR"-GAZE?

Show your skill with locating points on a four-quadrant grid. If you get all the locations right, you'll create a visual clue to answer the riddle below.

Where might you spot a celebrity deer drinking a mocha java?

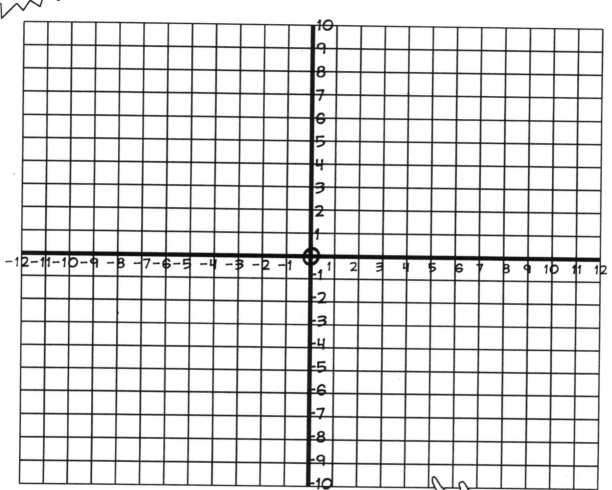

Plot each set of points and connect them in the order plotted.

A (−6, 9); (−5, 6); (−2, 6); (−4, 4); (−3, 1); (−6, 3); (−9, 1); (−8, 4); (−10, 6); (−7, 6); (−6, 9)

B (3, 1); (−1, 1); (−1, −2); (3, −2); (3, −5); (−1, −5)

C (1, 2); (−1, −6)

D (3, 2); (1, −6)

E (8, −4); (6, −4); (6, −6); (8, −6); (8, −8); (6, −8)

WHAT'S UNIQUE ABOUT A STREAK?

In the world of sports, certain athletes have had amazing streaks of wins or other great accomplishments. Take on a math challenge related to the streaks of four athletes.

Read each story. Use the elements on the sports shape to form an equation that can help to find the missing numbers. When you use an element, color the shape. (The information on a shape can be used more than once.)

1. Martina Navratilova

won 74 consecutive World Tennis Association matches. This is the sum of two consecutive even numbers. What are these numbers?

_____

2. Mike Vanderjagt

holds the record for kicking the most consecutive field goals (42) without missing. This number is equal to the sum of three consecutive integers that differ by three. What are these numbers?

_____

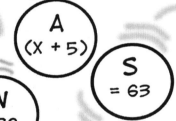
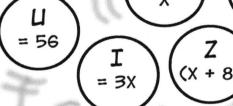
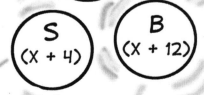

N (X + 1)

C +

T = 42

R 8X

O (X + 16)

P (X + 3)

F (X + 2)

A (X + 5)

S = 63

Y =74

M (X + 6)

E X

W = 36

U = 56

I = 3X

Z (X + 8)

S (X + 4)

B (X + 12)

3. Joe DiMaggio

holds the record (56 games), for the most consecutive baseball games played wherein he got at least one hit. Fifty-six is also the sum of four consecutive multiples of four. What are these numbers?

_____

4. Orel Hersheiser

holds the major league baseball record for pitching the most consecutive scoreless innings (63). This is the sum of three consecutive integers that differ by three. What are these numbers?

_____

Bonus

Find the shapes that are not colored. Notice the letters on those shapes. Unscramble those letters to finish the phrase below.

A streak is unique because these great feats happen

— — —   — —   — — —!

Name_____

WHOSE FINGERNAILS ARE THOSE?

The Guinness Book of Records is a wonderful compendium of outrageous statistics and wacky achievements by people who work to set records. To find the names of some of the champions—and their feats—evaluate these numerical expressions. Each solution yields a number fact connected to one Guinness record. Find the solution on the ribbon. The letter next to the solution will lead you to the name of the record-holder. Write the number of the problem on the big letter.

ASHRITA FURMAN   HANS LANGSETH   JOEY CHESTNUT   KIM SEUNG DO   FRANCISCO PEINADO TOLEDO

1. the longest fingernails (in ft)

$8\frac{4}{6} + 5(3\frac{1}{6})$

2. record amount of glass and metal eaten in a year (in lbs)

$(\frac{2}{3} \cdot 240) - \frac{1}{2}(5 \cdot 40)$

3. the greatest number of live poisonous snakes held in a person's mouth at one time

$5(1\frac{1}{2}) + \frac{1}{2}$

4. the longest beard (in ft)

$4 \cdot 3\frac{1}{3} + 4\frac{1}{6}$

5. the greatest length of time someone balanced on one foot (in hrs)

$(7 \cdot 13) - 15\frac{1}{3}$

6. most hot dogs eaten in 12 minutes

$(9\frac{1}{3} \cdot 6) + (2\frac{1}{2} \cdot 4)$

7. number of body piercings on woman who holds the record

$(\frac{6}{5})(1250)$

8. weight of 23 milk crates balanced on a chin for 11.23 seconds (in lbs)

$4(\frac{1}{9} \cdot 198)$

9. greatest number of tennis balls held in one hand

$5(3\frac{1}{5}) + (4 \cdot \frac{1}{2})$

10. number of minutes it took the first place winner to eat five watches

$6(16\frac{1}{3}) - (3 \cdot 1\frac{1}{3})$

H. 1500
E. 18   B. 17.5   C. 66
G. 60   F. $75\frac{2}{3}$ D. 94
A. 88   I. 8
J. $24\frac{1}{2}$

ARULANANTHAM SURESH JOACHIM   MICHEL LOTITO   ELAINE DAVIDSON   JACKIE BIBBY   LEE REDMOND

Name_____

WHAT'S THAT "WELL-ROUNDED" FIGURE?

Rounding solutions will lead you to the name of the favored figure that the baker is about to deliver to a fortunate customer. Solve each equation. **Round all solutions to the nearest whole number.** Find each answer in the puzzle and shade that wedge in the wheel.

1. $22x = 27.5$

Rounded solution _____

2. $2523 = 9x$

Rounded solution _____

3. $\frac{2801}{x} = 99$

Rounded solution _____

4. $\frac{x}{13} = 3$

Rounded solution _____

5. $19x = 360$

Rounded solution _____

6. $19{,}822 = 180x$

Rounded solution _____

7. $\frac{488}{19} = x$

Rounded solution _____

8. $98{,}008 = 1000x$

Rounded solution _____

9. $5460 = 260x$

Rounded solution _____

10. $30 = \frac{1230}{x}$

Rounded solution _____

11. $19x = 4749$

Rounded solution _____

12. $\frac{101}{21} = x$

Rounded solution _____

13. $60x = 3541$

Rounded solution _____

14. $5x = 3490$

Rounded solution _____

What is in the box? Take the letters from the wheels with correct answers. Write the letters in order of the values of the answers—from least to greatest.

___ ___ ___ ___ ___ ___ ___ ___ ___ ___ ___ ___ ___ ___

Name_____

WHERE IS THE MATCHING SQUARE?

Every square in the puzzle has one other square that matches it. Your job is to find the matching pairs. Follow the directions to color two squares in each color. Choose and use your formulas carefully. The puzzle can be tricky. (Use 3.14 as the value for π.)

a $113.04m^3$	b	c $62.8m^3$	d 16	e 10	f
g	h $62.8m$	i $110.04m^3$	j	k $94m^2$	l $12m^2$
m $24m$	n $60m^3$	o	p 8	q	r $188.4m^3$
s 6	t	u $324m^3$	v	w $144m^2$	x $125.6m$

Color the squares as directed:

RED: the rectangular prism; its surface area (w = 3m, l = 5m, h = 4 m)

BLUE: the sphere; its volume (r = 3 m)

GREEN: the cylinder; the sum of the lengths of its edges (r = 10 m)

ORANGE: the cube; number of its vertices

YELLOW: the triangular prism; the total area of its bases (base length = 2 m, height = 6 m)

PINK: the cone; its volume (r = 2 m, height = 15 m)

PURPLE: the pentagonal pyramid; the number of its faces

BROWN: the pyramid; its surface area (the base is a 6 m square; height of side = 9 m)

74 HAVE YOU WRESTLED WITH ALGEBRA?

A wrestler is put in a class according to his weight, and only competes against someone else in his class. Use your algebra skills to "wrestle" these facts into proportions. Then solve the proportions to find the weights of the wrestlers on the Wy High wrestling team. Write and solve a proportion to answer each question. Keep track of all the wrestlers' weights on the weight chart. Find and color a section in the puzzle for each weight.

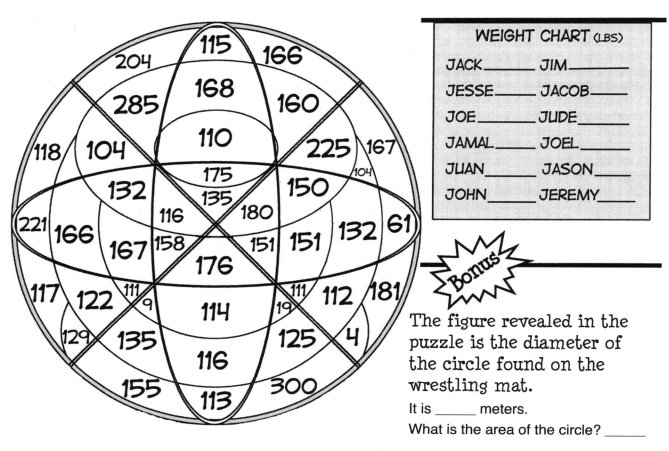

WEIGHT CHART (LBS)	
JACK_____	JIM_____
JESSE_____	JACOB_____
JOE_____	JUDE_____
JAMAL_____	JOEL_____
JUAN_____	JASON_____
JOHN_____	JEREMY_____

Bonus

The figure revealed in the puzzle is the diameter of the circle found on the wrestling mat.

It is _____ meters.

What is the area of the circle? _____

1. This proportion compares Jack's weight to Joe's: **26:28**. Jack weighs **104**. What is Joe's weight?

2. Juan's weight in comparison to Jason's is **27:32**. Jason weighs **160**. What is Juan's weight?

3. Jesse weighs **150**. A proportion that compares Jeremy's weight to Jesse's is **45:30**. How much does Jeremy weigh?

4. The ratio of Jacob's weight to Joel's is **57:25**. Jacob weighs **285**. What does Joel weigh?

5. Jim weighed **120**. He and Jamal both gained 12 pounds recently. Now Jim's weight compares to Jamal's in an **11:14** ratio. What did Jamal weigh before the weight gain?

6. Jude's weight compares to John's in a **45:29** ratio. John weighs **116**. What is Jude's weight?

7. The relationship of Jack's weight to the sum of five other wrestlers' weights is shown by the proportion $\frac{1}{9}$. Four of the wrestlers are Jacob, Jeremy, John, and Jesse. Who is the fifth wrestler?

Puzzle

15 WHO'S THE TALLEST OF THEM ALL?

Titan, Goliath, Dragster, Kingda Ka—who are these guys? They're some of the tallest steel roller coasters in the United States. Solve the word problems below and search for the answers in the number grid. The correct answers go left to right, top to bottom, or diagonally left to right.

1. The *Millennium Force* (Ohio) has a maximum height of 310 feet. *Titan* (Texas) is ten feet taller than *Goliath* (California) and the sum of their heights is 140 feet less than twice *Millennium Force's* height. How tall is *Titan* (in feet)?

2. *Kingda Ka's* (Tennessee) has a height 14 feet less than twice *Goliath's*. (Refer back to problem 1 to find *Goliath's* height.) How tall is *Kingda Ka* (in feet)?

3. *Top Thrill Dragster* (Ohio) is (1800% of 2) feet less than *Kingda Ka*. (Refer back to problem 2 for *Kingda Ka's* height.) How tall is *Top Thrill Dragster* (in feet)?

4. The ride on the *Titan* is twice as long as the ride on the *Millennium Force* and 30 seconds longer than the ride on *Goliath*. The sum for all three is 8 minutes 15 seconds. What is the length of the ride on *Titan* (in minutes)?

5. The height requirement in order to ride *Kingda Ka* is six inches less than it is to ride *Millennium Force*. The sum of the required heights for both rides is 102 inches. How tall must you be to ride *Millennium Force* (in feet)?

6. The maximum vertical angle on the *Millennium Force* is 19° more than on *Goliath*, and 15° more than *Titan's*. The sum of all three angles is 206°. What is the maximum vertical angle on *Goliath* (in degrees)?

4	7	$\frac{5}{8}$	3	6	0	2	$\frac{2}{3}$
$\frac{1}{2}$	9	0	2	4	9	3	3
8	5	2	1	4	6	4	3
7	4	0	$\frac{3}{4}$	9	5	1	$\frac{1}{3}$
$\frac{3}{8}$	2	1	2	4	7	6	2
4	0	6	2	5	2	$\frac{7}{10}$	0
3	9	3	$\frac{1}{2}$	7	$\frac{9}{15}$	8	5
7	$\frac{1}{8}$	4	5	5	6	2	$\frac{1}{2}$

Bonus Which of the five roller coasters is the tallest?

16 WHAT DID THE SPIDER SAY TO THE FLY?

To answer this question, you must first simplify some expressions. Simplify the expression in each outer segment of the web. Look for the correct simplification in one of the two smaller (inner) segments. When you find it, shade that segment.

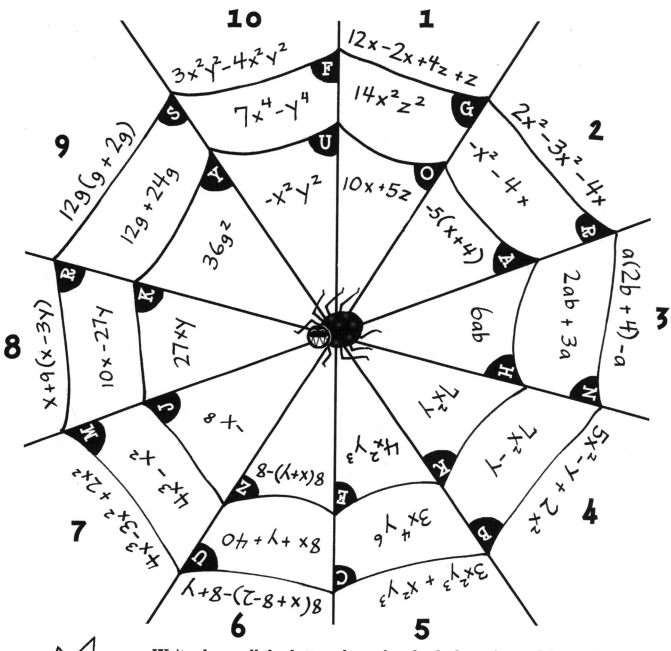

Write down all the letters from the shaded sections of the web. Then, unscramble the letters to answer the question in the title.

Riddle

What did the spider say to the fly?

"I've got ___ ___ ___ ___ ___ ___ ___ ___ ___ ___ ___ ___ !

Name_____

HOW WOULD YOU RATE THE TRIP?

northern border | Michigan | mile 394

Mackinaw Exit 348

Gaylord | Exit 282

Frankenmuth | Exit 144

MICHIGAN

Detroit Exit 51

Temperance | Exit 5

northern Ohio | border mile 210

Sylvania | Exit 204

OHIO | Bowling Green State University Exit 181

Dayton Exit 53

Cincinnati Exit 2

northern | Kentucky border mile 194

Florence Exit 181

KENTUCKY

Lexington Exit 113

Berea Exit 77

southern Kentucky | border

I-75 is a north-south running Interstate that stretches from southern Florida to northern Michigan. In the states of Kentucky, Ohio, and Michigan, the exits are numbered in terms of miles from the southern border. Kentucky's northernmost exit is Exit 194, Ohio's is 210, and Michigan's is 394. Use this information and the map to solve the rate problems.

(Y) 1. Jenny lives by the Lexington, KY, Exit **113** and heads for the Florence Mall at Exit **181**. She travels at an average rate of **60** mph. How long will the trip take? (Round to the nearest hour). _____

(I) 2. Jim goes to school in Berea, KY, and wishes to visit a friend in Bowling Green, OH. The trip takes him **4** hours and **56** minutes. What is his rate of travel? _____ mph

(X) 3. Sammi lives in Sylvania, OH, and wants to go skiing in Gaylord, MI. She travels the distance at **60** mph. How long will the trip take (in minutes)?

(N) 4. Bob, from Berea, KY, decides to go skiing up in Gaylord, MI, as well. How long does his trip take, if he travels at **60** mph? (Round to the nearest hour.)

(F) 5. Frank, from Frankenmuth, MI, heads for a basketball game at the University of Kentucky in Lexington. He travels the distance in **7** hours. What is his average rate of travel (rounded to nearest whole number)? _____ mph

(T) 6. Terry drives from Temperance, MI, to Detroit, MI, then back to Cincinnati, OH (Exit **2**). If she travels at **60** mph, can she do the trip in less than **6** hours?

(S) 7. Mac drives from Lexington, KY, to Mackinaw, MI. The speed limit is **65** mph on most of his trip. Can he make the trip in **8** hours if he does not exceed the speed limit?

Puzzle

Place the letter at the front of the problem above any spaces that have its answer.

Most of the drivers seem to think that

___ ___ ___ ___ ___   ___ ___   ___ ___ ___ ___ ___ ___
no   60   288   yes   1   60   no   10   60   62   yes   1

Name_____

CAN THERE BE MULTIPLE WINNERS?

Four knights race through an enchanted forest, competing to find golden apples for a princess. Multiples of each knight's number are strewn about the forest. Draw a path for each knight that goes through objects with his multiples. The goal is to be the first to reach the apple with his number.

7 _____

3 _____

4 _____

5 ____

$2\sqrt{196}$

$3^2 + 15$

$\sqrt{64}$

800

918

256

7^3

525

$2^5 + 1$

4

275

$-5 + \sqrt{10,000}$

77

$\sqrt{625}$

420

972

$2^4 + 2^3 + 1$

$\sqrt{144}$

$11^2 + 5$

$2^6 - 1$

369

44

5

7

3

4

Puzzle

The winner is the racer who got to the finish line with the fewest number of stops.

1. Are there multiple winners? _____ Who? _____

2. One of the objects holds a multiple of all four numbers. What is the object?

Name_____

WHERE ARE THOSE MISSING STATS?

Southwest High School is proud of a volleyball team with eight girls who rotate on the varsity squad. The table shows their statistics from a recent tournament. The problem is—the stats are not written in their usual form. They are written as powers or roots of numbers. Furthermore, a few stats are missing. Evaluate each expression and write the value near the expression.

PLAYER	HITS	DIGS	ASSISTS	ACES	BLOCKS
SARAH	$\sqrt{1}$	$0(\sqrt{144})$	$\sqrt{80+20}$	$\sqrt[3]{64}$	1^2
SUSAN	$(\sqrt{4}+\sqrt{9})-5$		$1^2+\sqrt{4}$	-2^2	$\sqrt{49}$
SIERRA	2^3	$\sqrt[4]{81}$	$\sqrt{49}-4$	$-4+(-2)^2$	$\sqrt[8]{256}$
SAMANTHA	$\sqrt[4]{16}$	2^4-4^2	-3^2-6	9^2-6^2-41	$\sqrt{25}-\sqrt{4}$
STACEY	$\sqrt{0}$	$\sqrt{9}$	$\sqrt[3]{125}$	$\sqrt[3]{64}$	2^4-4^2
STEPHANIE	$\sqrt[3]{8}$	$\sqrt{100}-\sqrt{16}$	$\sqrt{121}-\sqrt{100}$	7^2-45	
SASHA	$2(2^2)$	0^4	-1^2	$\sqrt{9}+\sqrt{1}$	$\sqrt{60-11}$
CECILIA		$\sqrt[6]{64}$	$\sqrt{36}$	$\sqrt{4} \cdot \sqrt[3]{8}$	-1^4

1. The sums of the completed columns and rows have something in common. Each sum is a multiple of a particular number. This number is _____ .

2. Knowing the answer to number #2 above, figure out which stats are missing. Each of these fits into one of the spaces. Which ones belong where?

$$\sqrt[3]{27} \qquad\qquad \sqrt[5]{32} \qquad\qquad 6^2-29$$

Name_____

HOW OMINOUS IS THE DATE?

The system of Roman numerals was probably used by Julius Caesar, an influential leader of the Roman Empire. Find the missing variables from these Roman equations. Connect the dots by the answers in the order of the problems. This will form a picture related to Julius Caesar. Use the last two solutions to find a date that has a connection to Julius Caesar.

Solve each equation for n.

1. n + V = LXXX

2. n − XXV = XVI

3. CIII − X(n) = XXXIII

4. CCLV − CCXC = n

5. n − CMLXXXIV = −LXXXIV

6. MDLV + n = MDC

7. MXIV − VII = n + D

8. DXXV − DXLV = n

9. n(CMXXX) = MDCCCLX

10. CDII − n = CCCLXII

11. n − CXCII = VIII

12. (III + CDXCVII)n = MMD

13. MMC + n = MMCDXC

14. CCCXXXIII ÷ n = CXI

15. (−CCI)n + MMM = −XV

16. MDXL + n = MCDXCVI

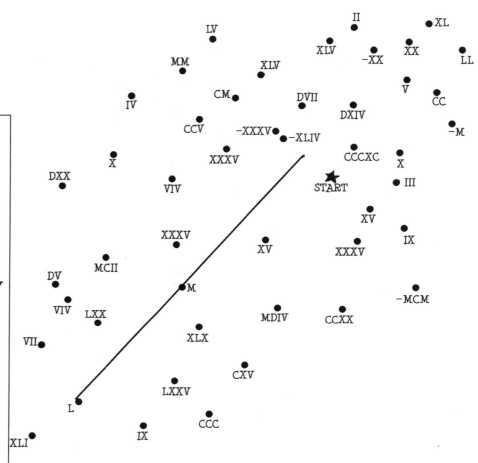

Write Arabic number solutions from the last three problems to form a date:

_____ / _____ / _____BC

What is ominous about the date?

Name_____

Puzzle It! Pre-Algebra Riddles   26   ©*Incentive Publications, Inc., Nashville, TN.*

WHO WAS DREAMIN' OF CALIFORNIA?

Throughout the past and present in America, many people and groups have dreamed of a life in California. Solve this puzzle to find the name of one group that headed west in search of a particular dream.

Solve the equations. Find each solution on the grid and shade in the squares it covers. **Begin each answer with a $ sign.** Answers can be top to bottom or horizontal left to right only. Some may overlap. Also, SHADE ALL ZEROS.

1	2	6	$	2	8	7	4	9	4	9	2	6	4	$	1	$	2	3	$	2
4	$	3	$	3	$	0	$	$	$	$	2	$	7	8	5	4	$	3	$	6
7	6	5	1	6	6	2	9	2	$	3	$	3	7	9	$	2	2	7	1	8
2	0	5	2	5	5	5	2	7	7	5	2	6	6	6	3	8	9	$	2	6
8	$	9	9	6	4	$	8	6	$	3	3	$	$	4	9	6	$	0	0	5
9	2	5	0	$	3	2	$	3	0	1	4	2	9	5	$	$	0	4	$	5
4	6	3	$	3	8	5	7	8	$	0	5	6	$	2	4	$	2	0	5	6
6	1	9	5	2	$	3	6	6	2	5	8	8	4	0	$	$	1	5	0	9
$	$	3	0	2	3	4	5	3	1	$	5	4	0	9	0	2	0	0	6	$
3	$	7	5	1	$	3	9	6	6	5	9	7	$	2	6	1	$	6	1	2

1. $x \div \frac{1}{8} = \$480$ x = _____
2. $\frac{12}{3}x = \$32$ x = _____
3. $\$87 + (-x) = \$54$ x = _____
4. $\$19.80 = 0.2x$ x = _____
5. $\$10 + \frac{1}{2}x = \$34.50$ x = _____
6. $7(x^2) = \$112$ x = _____
7. $x = \$30^2 + \$28$ x = _____
8. $x^2 = \$15^2 - \$12^2$ x = _____
9. $x \div 43 = \$30$ x = _____
10. $\$14 = \frac{2}{3}x$ x = _____

11. $\$40,000 \div x = \$800$ x = _____
12. $x - (-\$20) + x(\$6) = \$55$ x = _____
13. $32x - \$928 = 2(\$100^2)$ x = _____
14. $45x = (4 \cdot \$8,600) + 5^2$ x = _____

15. Working $2\frac{1}{2}$ hours a day, a prospector finds an amount of gold equal to $4 an hour. He needs to get gold of **x** value, and he plans to work 4 days to get it. How much does he need?

x = _____

Bonus

The name of this California dreamin' group is _____.

Find out why they came to California.

IS SAM HEADED FOR DISASTER?

Sam is known in the area as the "King of Slalom." Today, he's off on a race to defend his title as the champion. But does he make it to the finish line? When Sam comes to an intersection (labeled with a large letter), find the sign with that letter and solve the inequality. Choose the path for Sam that has the correct solution to that problem. Use a colored pen to follow his trail.

These characters from history have something in common. Solve the equations to figure it out. Write the value of the variable on the "paper" below the equation. Note that each person's birth date (year) appears as a part of the equation.

1. Einstein

$1879 \textcircled{t} = 939\frac{1}{2}$

2. Sophie Germain

$1776 \textcircled{m} = 4144$

3. Leonard Euler

$1707 \div \textcircled{a} = 17.07$

4. Euclid

$\frac{300}{\textcircled{e}} = 200$

5. John Venn

$1834 - (\textcircled{n}) = 2000$

6. Blaise Pascal

$5.41 \textcircled{s} = 1623$

7. Hippocrates

$460 \textcircled{h} = 345$

8. Plato

$424 = 53 \textcircled{t}$

9. Isaac Newton

$41^2 - \textcircled{i} = 1643$

10. Archimedes

$287 \textcircled{m} = 2.87$

11. Florence Nightingale

$220 - 89 \textcircled{i} = -1560$

12. Pythagoras

$\textcircled{a} = \frac{580}{5800}$

13. Descartes

$53\frac{1}{5} \textcircled{c} = 1596$

14. Shakuntala Devi

$1939 = 323\frac{1}{6} \textcircled{a}$

Puzzle

Use the circled letters to find out what they have in common. Each letter is the variable from one of the equations. Write these circled letters below **in order of their value from least to greatest**. (You'll have to pay attention to the solutions!)

___ ___ ___ ___ ___ ___ ___ ___ ___ ___ ___ ___ ___ ___

Name_____

WHEN IS SUBSTITUTION A GOOD IDEA?

Substitution has many uses. In sports, the coach sends players into the game to substitute for another player who needs a rest. The substitution makes a difference in the success of the game. In math equations, a number gets substituted for a letter variable. The value of that number makes a great difference in the solution to the problem.

Make the substitutions to solve the equations.

A = 1	
B = $3\frac{1}{2}$	
D = −2	
E = 0	
H = 40	
I = 10	
M = −4	
N = 45	
O = $\frac{1}{8}$	
S = 17	
T = 400	
U = −19	

A. Substitute: $a = \frac{1}{2}$
$b = 2$
$c = 0$
$d = -3$
$e = 4$

1. $ab + (cd)^e =$ _____

2. $a + b + c + d + e =$ _____

3. $a^b e + d =$ _____

4. $(a + b)c =$ _____

B. Substitute: $f = 4$
$g = -4$
$h = \frac{1}{2}$
$i = -1\frac{1}{2}$
$j = 10$

5. $fghij =$ _____

6. $f + g + h + i + j =$ _____

7. $gh + if =$ _____

8. $fj - ij =$ _____

9. $h^f + i^f =$ _____

C. Substitute: $p = 10$; $q = 2$; $r = 4$; $s = 1$; $t = \frac{1}{2}$

10. $q^r + s =$ _____

11. $rp^q =$ _____

12. $(q + s)^r - p^q =$ _____

The problem numbers are beneath the lines in the puzzle. Use the key to find each problem's solution. Translate the solution into a capital letter. Write the letter into the puzzle above the problem number—and finish the conversation about substitution.

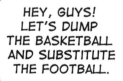

GET IN THERE AND MAKE THE SUBSTITUTION!

HEY, GUYS! LET'S DUMP THE BASKETBALL AND SUBSTITUTE THE FOOTBALL.

HEY! THAT WAS

$\overline{8}$ $\overline{9}$ $\overline{11}$　$\overline{11}$ $\overline{5}$ $\overline{4}$　$\overline{10}$ $\overline{12}$ $\overline{2}$ $\overline{10}$ $\overline{11}$ $\overline{6}$ $\overline{11}$ $\overline{12}$ $\overline{11}$ $\overline{6}$ $\overline{9}$ $\overline{8}$

$\overline{6}$　$\overline{5}$ $\overline{1}$ $\overline{3}$　$\overline{6}$ $\overline{8}$　$\overline{7}$ $\overline{6}$ $\overline{8}$ $\overline{3}$.

Name_____

WHAT DID THE SNAIL SAY TO THE WAITER?

Answer this pressing question by translating word expressions into numbers and symbols. Write each translation into the puzzle. Write each element in a separate square. For instance, $4x^2 - y = 3$ would take FIVE squares ($4x^2$; $-$; y; $=$; 3).

The puzzle is tricky! The answers overlap. Watch the numbers before each problem. These show you where to place the answer.

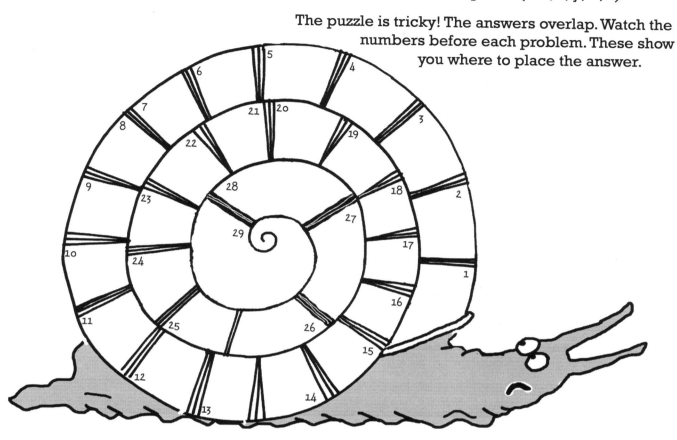

1–5. The sum of a number **(n)** and six times another number **(c)** is less than four times a third number **(g)**.	5–11. Four times a number **(g)** is equal to eighty less the sum of five times a number **(a)** squared and negative five times another number **(v)**.	11–15. Negative five times a number **(v)** less ninety is equal to the negative of a number **(o)** squared.
15–19. A negative number **(o)** squared combined with 70 is equal to three times another number **(t)**.	19–25. Three times a number **(t)** divided by ten times another number **(d)** is equal to the sum of another number **(e)** and twenty.	23–29. The sum of a number **(e)** and twenty is greater than twice another number **(s)** less nine times a third number **(r)**.

Under each blank, find a number from a square in the puzzle. Go to that square and notice the letter used as the variable. Write that letter in the blank.

The snail's plea to the waiter was

___ ___ ___ , ___   ___ ___ ___ ___ ___   ___ ___ ___ ___ ___ ___ ___ ___ ___!
21   15   1   19   27   23   29   11   23   23   27   3   9   29   5   15   19

DO THE SOCKS TELL THE STORY?

A sock drawer can tell a lot about probability. Just ask a question about what might happen when someone reaches in for a pair of socks and write a ratio about probable outcomes. Solve each probability problem with a ratio. Look in the sock drawer (below). Find all the socks with that solution. Color the sock in the color shown for the section.

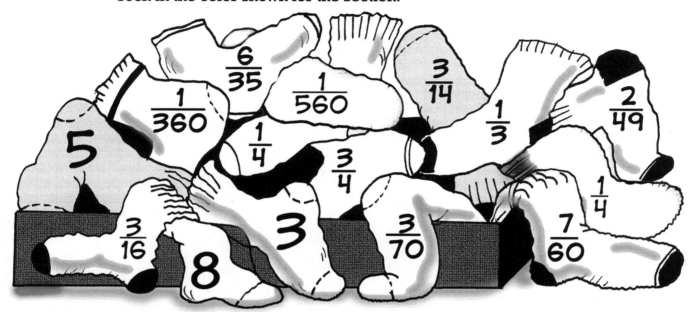

Color the answer-socks RED for problems 1 and 2.
> A dryer holds 12 socks. Eight are black (B). One is red (R). The rest are white (W). Jerome reaches in (without looking) and grabs one.

1. P (W) =   **2. P (not B) =**

Color the answer-socks BLUE for problems 3 and 4.
> Trevor's soccer bag holds lots of socks: 4 red (R), 7 green (G), 3 white (W), and 2 purple (P).

3. He takes 2 socks. **P(R and G) =**   **4.** He replaces 2 and takes 3. **P (3W) =**

Color the answer-socks GREEN for problems 5–7.
> A laundry basket holds 21 socks. Nine are green (G). Two are red (R). The rest are black (B). Michelle grabs two socks.

5. P (pair of B) =   **6. P (G, R) =**   **7. P (pair of G) =**

Color the answer-socks YELLOW for problem 8.
> **8.** Abby's drawer has 18 blue (B) socks and four white (W) socks. How many socks will she have to take out to be certain that she will have a matching pair?

Bonus

Look at the sock drawer you have colored. If you reached into this drawer without looking and grabbed two socks, what is the probability that you would get a pair of white socks?

Name _____

HOW'S YOUR JOB, SIR?

A reporter interviews a roller-coaster engineer to learn about the challenges and rewards of his job. To find the engineer's answer to one of the questions, evaluate these expressions with powers. You'll also learn some interesting information about the height, speed, or length of these major roller coasters in Japan. They are some of the highest, fastest steel coasters in the world.

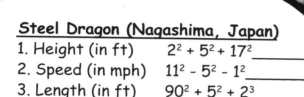

Steel Dragon (Nagashima, Japan)
1. Height (in ft) $2^2 + 5^2 + 17^2$ _____
2. Speed (in mph) $11^2 - 5^2 - 1^2$ _____
3. Length (in ft) $90^2 + 5^2 + 2^3$ _____

Thunder Dolphin (Tokyo, Japan)
4. Height (in ft) $17^2 - 5^2 - 1^2$ _____
5. Speed (in mph) 3^4 _____
6. Length (in ft) $60^2 - 10^2$ _____

Fujiyama (Fujiyoshida, Japan)
7. Height (in ft) $3^2 + 5^2 + 15^2$ _____
8. Speed (in mph) $6^2 + 7^2 - 2^2$ _____
9. Length (in ft) $80^2 + 18^2 - 4^2$ _____

A	D	G	I
318	259	249	263
N	O	P	S
95	81	78	8133
T	U	W	
6708	3500	3782	

Eejanaika (Fujiyoshida, Japan)
10. Height (in ft) $15^2 + 5^2 - 1^2$ _____
11. Speed (in mph) $3^4 - 3^1$ _____
12. Length (in ft) $60^2 + 10^2 + 9^2 + 1^2$ _____

Beneath each blank is the number of a problem. Use the key to find the matching letter for the solution to that problem. Write the letter in the blank.

Reporter to roller-coaster engineer: "How do you feel about your job?"

Roller-coaster engineer: "Oh . . .

___ ___ ___   ___ ___ ___   ___ ___ ___
4   9   3   10   8   9   4   9   3

___ ___ ___   ___ ___ ___   ___ ___ ___ ___ ___ !"
6 11   3   1   2   7   7   5 12   2   3

Name_____

28 | IS THIS A NEW ANGLE ON TIME?

When a clock is a circle, it gives you a chance to puzzle about angles and other measurements. These circular clocks will help you solve a riddle about time if you add your knowledge about the measurements in a circle.

Assume that the hour hand is 3 inches long and the minute hand is 4 inches long.

Clock # 1

1. Through how much area (in²) has the minute hand swept since 12:30? **(G)**
2. How many degrees has the minute hand moved since 11:30? **(A)**
3. How long (min) will it be before the two hands form an angle of 198°? **(I)**

Clock # 2

4. How many inches has the tip of the minute hand traveled since 1:30? **(C)**
5. How many degrees has the hour hand moved since 9:30? **(S)**
6. When the hour hand moves another 180°, what time will it be? **(L)**

Clock # 3

7. How many degrees has the minute hand moved since 9:00? **(D)**
8. Through how much area (in²) has the minute hand swept since 6:40? **(O)**
9. When the hour hand moves another 90°, what time will it be? **(T)**

Clock # 4

10. How many degrees will the minute hand move to reach a time of 8:30? **(N)**
11. How many inches has the tip of the minute hand moved since 1:20? **(U)**
12. When the tip of the minute hand moves another 47.1 in, what time will it be? **(E)**

Clock # 5

13. What time will it be when the minute hand has moved another 810°? **(H)**
14. How many degrees has the hour hand moved since noon? **(M)**

Riddle

Place the letter at the end of each problem above the answer below.
If the answer is not there, skip to the next problem.

When it's noon in Greenwich, England (at the Prime Meridian), what time is it?

_____ _____ _____ _____ _____   _____ _____ _____ _____
3:30 188.4 420 50.24 8:45   12:10 33 195 8:50

Name_____

WHO TOOK THE TACOS?

When Detective Samantha Sly got to the scene of the crime, she found three clues. Follow the clues to help her track down the main suspect.

The Mystery

Maria and Eduardo, owners of the Taco Benito, prepared dozens of tacos, then locked up the place and took a quick walk in the park before the busy lunch hour. When they returned, the restaurant was in shambles. The cash drawer had not been touched, but all the tacos—in twelve different varieties—were gone. Maria and Eduardo called the police.

Detective Sly found three clues:

#1 a set of unsolved math equations
#2 a key matching math solutions to the twelve varieties of missing tacos
#3 a piece of paper with blank lines

Directions:

In Clue # 1, round all numbers to the nearest whole number. Solve each equation. Find its answer on the key for Clue # 2. Find the **underlined** letter in the matching taco description. Write this letter above the line in Clue # 3 that has the number of that problem.

Clue #1

1. $5.1x = 249.8$

2. $4.99 \div x = 5$

3. $(-8.8)(4.9) = x$

4. $-5.4x = 85$

5. $-120 \div x = 119.06$

6. $15.02x = 120$

7. $(14.9)(5.11) = x$

8. $-35 = -4.98x$

9. $x \div 4.8 = -10.9$

10. $(-9.9)(11.2) = x$

11. $x \div (-16) = -5.1$

12. $(.9)(x^2) = 100$

Clue #2   KEY

-55 = sliced eggpl<u>a</u>nt
10 = spicy <u>b</u>ologna
75 = re<u>d</u> onions
-17 = chopped cabba<u>g</u>e
-1 = <u>f</u>ried snails
50 = crawfi<u>s</u>h
-110 = <u>i</u>ce cream
8 = <u>l</u>eafy spinach
80 = gree<u>n</u> tomatoes
-45 = shredded p<u>o</u>rk
1 = cream chee<u>s</u>e
7 = lobster <u>t</u>ail

Clue #3

$$\overline{}_{8} \ \overline{}_{1} \ \overline{}_{4}$$

$$\overline{}_{2} \ \overline{}_{9} \ \overline{}_{6} \ \overline{}_{2} \ \overline{}_{9}$$

$$\overline{}_{12} \ \overline{}_{9} \ \overline{}_{11} \ \overline{}_{7} \ \overline{}_{10} \ \overline{}_{8} \ \overline{}_{3}$$

Name_____

WILL THE SHIP FIND ITS WAY?

A cargo spaceship has just left the space station, headed for a new colony. It must navigate through a maze of space bodies, picking up supplies as it goes. Find the correct scientific notation for each standard notation number on the rocket stop list. Draw a line to connect the correct answers in order. As you follow the ship's progress, pick up a letter at each stop. Then unscramble the letters to find the name of the spaceship.

Rocket Stops for Supplies
(in order)

1. 143,000
   (for fuel)

2. 14,300,000
   (for salt)

3. 143
   (for food)

4. .00143
   (for lumber)

5. .143
   (for helium)

6. 1,430,000
   (for iron)

7. 1.43
   (for dry ice)

8. 1430
   (by mistake)

9. 143,000,000
   (for medicine)

10. .0143
    (for livestock)

11. 14.3
    (destination)

n 1.43×10^7

u 14.3×10^{15}

b 14.3×10^{-25}

p $.143 \times 10^2$

m 1.43×10^6

g 1.43×10^5

f 1.43×10^3

c 1.43×10^8

a 1.43×10^{-3}

r 143×10^8

t 1.43×10^{-1}

s 1.43×10^9

i 1.43×10^0

e 1.43×10^{-2}

i 1.43×10^2

n 1.43×10^1

h 143×10^8

d 14.3×10^{20}

Puzzle

Unscramble the letters you've picked up to find the name of the mystery ship: It's not the <u>Enterprise</u> or the <u>Intrepid</u>. It's

The ___ ___ ___ ___ ___ ___ ___ ___ ___ ___ ___

Name _____

IS THERE ORDER IN THE STARBURST?

Look for ordered pairs that can solve the equation in the center of the starburst. Each "arm" of the starburst holds three numbers. On some of the arms, two of the three make up an ordered pair (**x, y**) that can satisfy the equation in the center. Find these pairs and shade the circles holding the numbers. Label the two numbers **x** and **y** correctly.

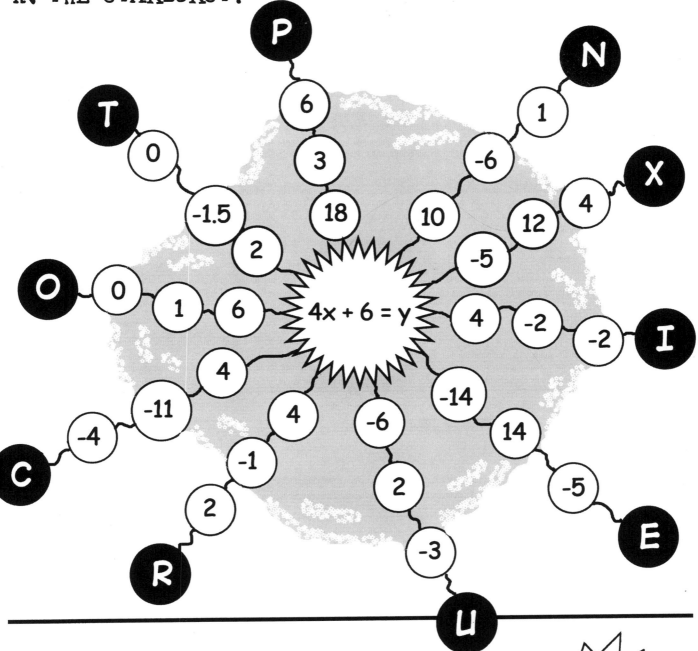

Take the letters from the outer ends of all the arms that have shaded circles. Unscramble these letters to create a word that describes what might cause a starburst.

____ ____ ____ ____ ____ ____ ____ ____

CAN YOU SEE ANOTHER ANGLE?

Some measurements for angles in the figures are written beneath the blank lines. However, some measurements are missing. Find the measurements for all the angles. Then use them to solve the riddle below.

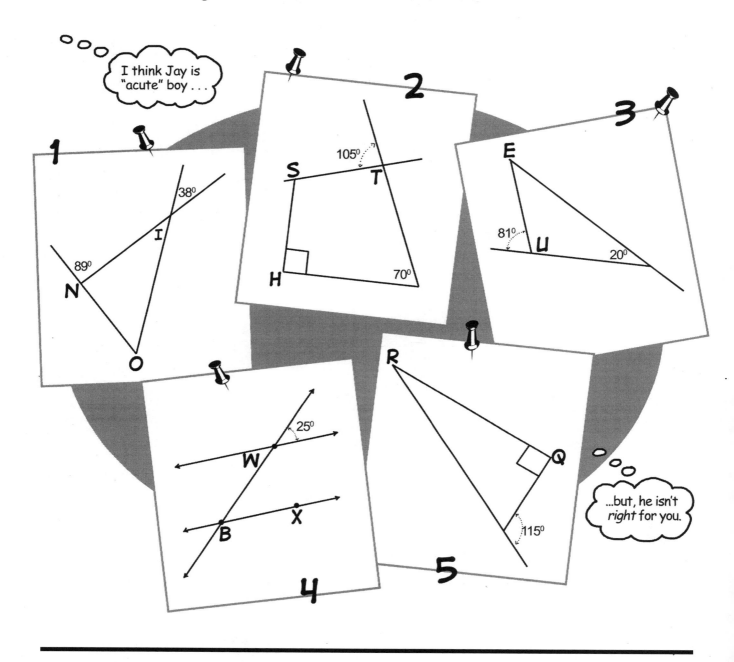

When does a "cute" angle cease to be cute?

___ ___ ___ ___   ___ ___ ___ ,   ___ ___ ___ ___ ___ ___
25° 90° 61° 91°   38° 75° 125°   51° 155° 75° 99° 125° 61°

WHAT'S IN THE BULL'S EYE?

Solve the target puzzle to find what is in the bull's eye. Notice that each "wedge" section has a letter variable. Those letters lead to the answer, but to find it, you must first find the values of the variables.

Start with the innermost letter or number of any section. Move outward, performing the operation given in the second ring to get the amount in the outer ring. The first section clockwise from "noon" would make up an equation $C - 12 = 3$. Solve this. Work around the circle until you have found the value for all the letter variables. Write the answers outside the target.

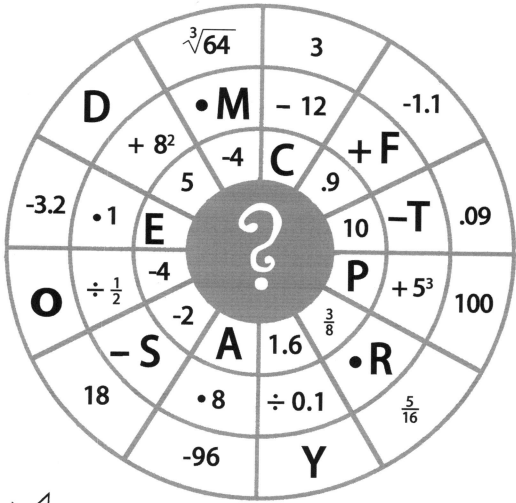

Puzzle

To find out what's in the bull's eye, write the letter from the target section that matches the value beneath the line.

___ ___ ___ ___ ___ ___ ___ ___   ___ ___ ___ ___
−1 −12 9.91 −12 69 −8 $\frac{5}{6}$ −20   15 −12 −25 −3.2

Name_____

WHICH PUZZLE IS EASIER?

Both puzzles check your understanding of concepts related to pre-algebra. But which one can you finish most quickly? Set a timer or check a clock. Keep track of the time it takes to finish each puzzle.

Across

4. −5 and 5 are _____
6. line which touches a curve at only one point
7. a number times itself
9. numbers and variables in expressions
10. circumference ÷ diameter

Down

1. number that yields a given product when multiplied by itself
2. two perpendicular lines with a common origin
3. number that tells the power
5. angle between 90° and 180°
8. comparison of two amounts

Across

1. part of a circle between two points on the circle
4. distance ÷ time
5. angle less than 90°
6. statistical figures or facts
7. 5-sided figure
8. triangle with no equal sides

Down

1. surface covered by a figure
2. middle number in a set of data
3. not = and not <
6. measurement unit of an angle

TIME FOR PUZZLE ONE: _____

TIME FOR PUZZLE TWO: _____

Name_____

Puzzle 35 WHO'S THE GREAT GEOMETRY FAN?

Graph some linear equations and solve a puzzle at the same time. If you plot the lines correctly, the letters of a name will be revealed. This is the name of one of the world's all-time greatest fans of geometry.

Look at each equation carefully. Use the small table to write three ordered pairs for the equation. Graph the pairs. Extend the line out beyond the graph until it "pierces" one (or more) capital letters. Circle these letters.

1 $x + y = 5$

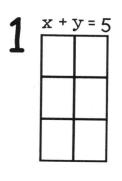

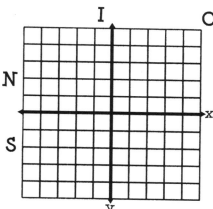

2 $x - y = 3$

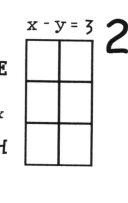

3 $y = 2x - 1$

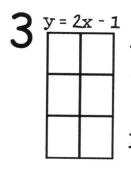

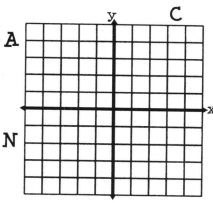

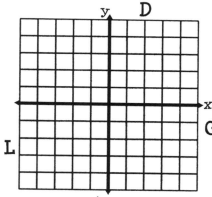

4 $y = x + 3$

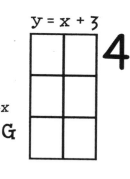

5 $x + y = 7$

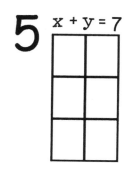

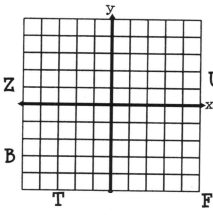

Puzzle

To find the name of one of the greatest geometry fans of all times, write down all the capital letters that are pierced by the lines you've graphed. UNSCRAMBLE these letters.

_____ _____ _____ _____ _____

Name_____

      41

Puzzle 36

WHERE DOES IT FIT ON THE TIMELINE?

Figure out the dates that match some key events in world history. Then use the dates to solve a puzzle that describes the goal of the activity.

Solve each equation to find a date. Then take a good look at all the dates. Write them on the timeline in the appropriate places.

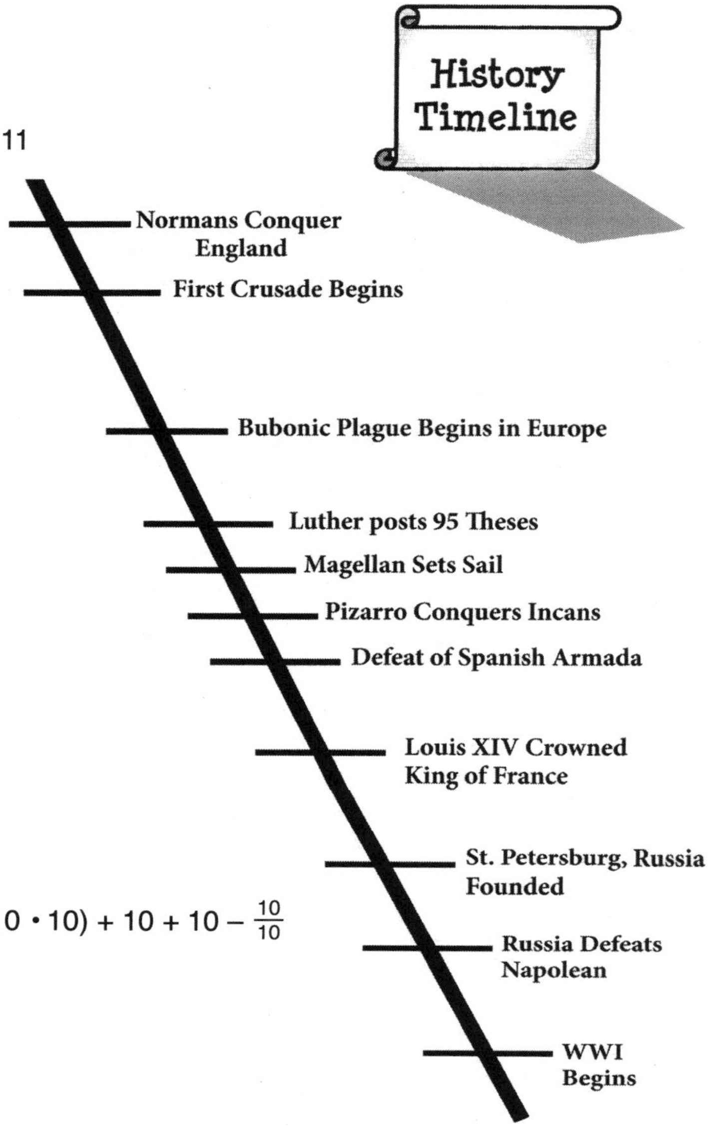

History Timeline
Normans Conquer England
First Crusade Begins
Bubonic Plague Begins in Europe
Luther posts 95 Theses
Magellan Sets Sail
Pizarro Conquers Incans
Defeat of Spanish Armada
Louis XIV Crowned King of France
St. Petersburg, Russia Founded
Russia Defeats Napolean
WWI Begins

$D = (11)^{1+1+1} + (1+1)\,(11)^{1+1} + (1+1)^{1+1} + 11$

$E = (2+2)\,(22^2) - 22$

$G = (3+3)\,(333) - (3 \cdot 33) - (3 \cdot 3^3) - (3+3)$

$H = 4^4\,(4 + \frac{4+4}{4}) - 4$

$I = 555 + 555 - 55 + 5 + 5 + \frac{5}{5}$

$N = 666 + 666 + 6 \cdot 6 \cdot 6 - (6 \cdot 6) + 6 - \frac{6}{6}$

$O = (7+7)\,(77) + 7 + 7 + \frac{7+7+7}{7}$

$R = (\frac{8+8}{8})\,(888) - 8(8 + \frac{8}{8})$

$S = (9+9)\,(99 - \frac{9}{9} - \frac{9}{9}) - 99 - \frac{9+9+9+9}{9}$

$T = 10 \cdot 10 \cdot 10 + (10+10)\,(10+10+10) - (10 \cdot 10) + 10 + 10 - \frac{10}{10}$

$Y = 11 \cdot 11 \cdot 11 + 11 + \frac{11+11+11+11}{11}$

Bonus

What's the goal of this page?

To find out (after solving the equations), write the letter that has this value.

To ___ ___ ___   ___ ___ ___ ___ ___ ___ ___

1812 1914 1519   1532 1066 1643 1519 1095 1704 1346

___ ___   ___ ___ ___ ___ ___

1066 1517   1095 1704 1588 1914 1704

Name____

WHICH ROUTE SHOULD SHE CHOOSE?

Desert explorer Ceci Sands is lost in the center of a desert. There are several routes that will help her find her way. On each path, solve the system of equations to find an ordered pair of numbers (**x, y**). Then move around the outside path until you find that ordered pair. Write the number of the system of equations by the destination that it represents.

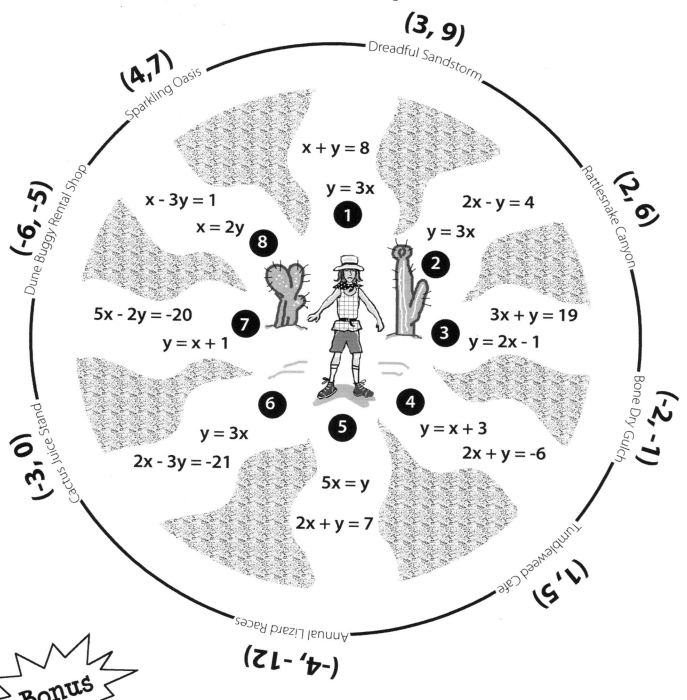

(3, 9) Dreadful Sandstorm

(4,7) Sparkling Oasis

(-6, -5) Dune Buggy Rental Shop

(2, 6) Rattlesnake Canyon

(-3, 0) Cactus Juice Stand

(-2, -1) Bone Dry Gulch

(-4, -12) Annual Lizard Races

(1, 5) Tumbleweed Café

$x + y = 8$
$y = 3x$
①

$2x - y = 4$
$y = 3x$
②

$x - 3y = 1$
$x = 2y$
⑧

$3x + y = 19$
$y = 2x - 1$
③

$5x - 2y = -20$
$y = x + 1$
⑦

$y = x + 3$
$2x + y = -6$
④

$y = 3x$
$2x - 3y = -21$
⑥

⑤

$5x = y$
$2x + y = 7$

Bonus

Which destination would you choose for Ceci?_____

Name_____

38

HOW LOW DO THE MULTIPLES GO?

Common multiples come in handy in math. Sometimes, the lower the
common multiple is, the better. Look in the column below each equation
to find the lowest common multiple for the terms in that equation.
When you find it, shade the square.

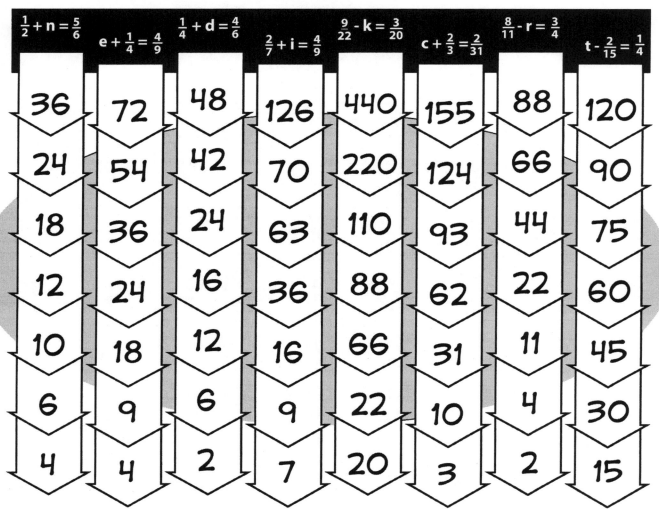

$\frac{1}{2} + n = \frac{5}{6}$	$e + \frac{1}{4} = \frac{4}{9}$	$\frac{1}{4} + d = \frac{4}{6}$	$\frac{2}{7} + i = \frac{4}{9}$	$\frac{9}{22} - k = \frac{3}{20}$	$c + \frac{2}{3} = \frac{2}{31}$	$\frac{8}{11} - r = \frac{3}{4}$	$t - \frac{2}{15} = \frac{1}{4}$
36	72	48	126	440	155	88	120
24	54	42	70	220	124	66	90
18	36	24	63	110	93	44	75
12	24	16	36	88	62	22	60
10	18	12	16	66	31	11	45
6	9	6	9	22	10	4	30
4	4	2	7	20	3	2	15

The Limbo, a famous (and fun) dance that originated in the Caribbean
region, requires the dancer to bend the body very low! Find another name
for this dance. Put the answers (shaded) in order from least to greatest—but
instead of writing numbers in the blanks below, use the letter of the variable
from the equation!

The Limbo is also called the **U** __ __ __ __   **S** __ __ __ __ dance.

WHICH EVIDENCE CRACKS THE CASE?

When Sgt. Sharif Sharpe, crime scene investigator, arrived at the scene of the break-in, he found several pieces of evidence. He collected all these and took them back to the lab. One of the clues contained equations. Find the solutions and use the key to crack the code below. This will help you figure out which piece or pieces of evidence really mattered in cracking the case.

Evidence List

fax
fingerprints
paper scrap
hair samples
crowbar
broken window
size 12 shoe prints
chocolate chip
cookie crumbs

The code for the combination to the safe with the payroll money is:

start with T; go clockwise to F; counter-clockwise to J; counter-clockwise to X; and clockwise to A.

FAX TRANSMISSION

Solve for x.

1. $x \div \frac{4}{5} = 11\frac{1}{4}$ x = _____ (U)

2. $2\frac{1}{8}x = 21\frac{1}{4}$ x = _____ (A)

3. $\left(\frac{6}{7}\right)\left(\frac{14}{6}\right) = x$ x = _____ (M)

4. $7\frac{3}{12} + x = 19\frac{1}{4}$ x = _____ (H)

5. $\frac{19}{3} - x = 6\frac{1}{3}$ x = _____ (T)

6. $x \div \frac{5}{8} = 6\frac{2}{5}$ x = _____ (X)

7. $2\frac{1}{9}x = 12\frac{2}{3}$ x = _____ (S)

8. $4x - 3\frac{7}{8} = 96\frac{1}{8}$ x = _____ (F)

9. $20\frac{1}{2}x = 164$ x = _____ (J)

10. $(2x) \div \frac{5}{3} = 13\frac{1}{5}$ x = _____ (E)

Puzzle

Fill each blank with the letter (from the FAX) associated with that solution.

___ ___ ___ ___ ___ ___ ___ ___ ___ ___ ___ ' ___ ___ ___
8 9 6 0   0 12 11   25 10 4   2 10 10 2

Bonus:
What is the safe's combination? ___ - ___ - ___ - ___ - ___

Name_____

Puzzle 40 — CAN IT BE A MISFORTUNE COOKIE?

If a fortune cookie has a "negative" message, would you call it a "mis"fortune cookie? These fortunes have expressions with negative exponents. Evaluate all the expressions. Then crack the code to read the advice from the big fortune cookie below.

$A = \left(-\frac{2}{3}\right)^{-1}$

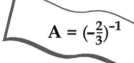

$B = \left(\frac{1}{3}\right)^{-3}$

$R = (-3)\left(\frac{1}{3}\right)^{-1}$

$E = (-4)^{-2}$

$C = 4^{-1}$

$M = (-1)^{-99}$

$H = (-2)\left(-\frac{1}{2}\right)^{-1}$

$G = \left(-\frac{1}{2}\right)^{-3}$

$T = \left(\frac{1}{12}\right)^{-2} \cdot 4^{-2}$

$F = (-2)^{-3}$

$Y = 4^{-1} - 2^{-1}$

$N = (-1)^{-100}$

$K = \left(\frac{1}{2}\right)^{-3}$

$I = -2 - \left(\frac{1}{2}\right)^{-1}$

$S = \left(\frac{1}{12}\right)^{-1} \cdot 4^{-1}$

$U = \left(\frac{1}{4}\right)^{-1} + \left(-\frac{1}{2}\right)^{-1}$

$O = 3 - \left(\frac{1}{3}\right)^{-1}$

$V = \left(1\frac{1}{2}\right)^{-1} \cdot \left(\frac{1}{9}\right)^{-1}$

Puzzle

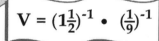

To find the "mis"fortune, write the letters from the equations on the blank lines below.

| 9 | −9 | $-\frac{1}{4}$ | | 1 | 0 | 9 | | 9 | 0 | | −8 | $\frac{1}{16}$ | 9 | | 9 | 0 | 0 |

| 1 | $\frac{1}{16}$ | −8 | $-1\frac{1}{2}$ | 9 | −4 | 6 | $\frac{1}{16}$ | | $-1\frac{1}{2}$ | 27 | 0 | 2 | 9 | | −1 | $-1\frac{1}{2}$ | 9 | 4 |

Name_____

DID YOU FOLLOW THE MONEY?

Follow the amounts of money to find a name that might be given to math students who are sharp with money problems. Write and solve an equation for each example. Then use the letter variables to solve the puzzle below.

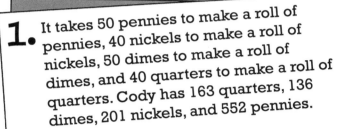

1. It takes 50 pennies to make a roll of pennies, 40 nickels to make a roll of nickels, 50 dimes to make a roll of dimes, and 40 quarters to make a roll of quarters. Cody has 163 quarters, 136 dimes, 201 nickels, and 552 pennies.

A. He can make _____ complete rolls of pennies.

B. He can make _____ complete rolls of nickels.

C. He can make _____ complete rolls of dimes.

D. He can make _____ complete rolls of quarters.

E. He has a total of _____ (amount of money rounded to the nearest whole dollar).

3. Jason collects dues for his school's Spanish Club. After a meeting where dues were paid, he had 20 fewer nickels than he did dimes, and two more dollar bills than he did dimes.
He also had 44 more quarters than dimes. The total amount collected was $96.00. Give the numbers of coins and bills.

L = number of dimes _____

N = number of nickels _____

Q = number of quarters _____

R = number of dollar bills _____

2. Megan has $2.45 in her purse. Along with ten pennies, she has one more dime than she does quarters, and three fewer nickels than quarters. Give the numbers of coins.

G = number of quarters _____

H = number of dimes _____

I = number of nickels _____

K = number of pennies _____

4. Nikki worked at the coat check at the basketball game to raise money for the team. In one hour, she collected a total of $12.40, all in quarters, dimes, and nickels. The number of nickels was two less than the number of dimes and the number of quarters was two more than the number of dimes. Give the numbers of coins.

S = number of nickels _____

T = number of dimes _____

U = number of quarters _____

Puzzle

Write the letter from the problem to match the solution.

To take care of money problems, pre-algebra students must become

_____ _____ _____ _____ _____ _____ _____ _____ _____ _____ _____
104   32   3   2   10   2   7   11   40   6   70

_____ _____ _____ _____ _____ _____ _____
11   62   30   3   28   30   28

IS IT ALL DOWNHILL FROM HERE?

The slope of a hill describes its steepness, just as the slope of a line measures its steepness on a graph. A line can have a positive or negative slope. Use your slope-finding skills to figure out which lines will take the skaters downhill.

For each equation, write the slope on the line in front of the number. Circle the numbers on the hill. Then draw a downhill path for the skateboarders. It must go THROUGH the numbers of problems with a negative slope (downhill) and AROUND other numbers.

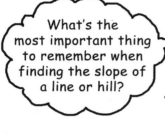

What's the most important thing to remember when finding the slope of a line or hill?

If you leave any banana peels on it, you'll have a slippery slope?

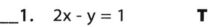

____	1.	2x - y = 1	T
____	2.	2x + 5y = 8	R
____	3.	y = -3x + 4	S
____	4.	-2y — 10 = -2x	A
____	5.	4x + y = 6	U
____	6.	-30 + 10y = -2x	V
____	7.	y = -1	D
____	8.	x + y = 0	N
____	9.	2x — 3y = 7	P
____	10.	3x + 20 = -4y	E
____	11.	3x + 2y = 6	O
____	12.	x + 2y = 8	I

Puzzle
Match each slope (beneath a blank) to the letter at the end of that equation.

No! It's more important to remember this:

$-\dfrac{2}{5}$ $-\dfrac{1}{2}$ -3 $-\dfrac{3}{4}$ $-\dfrac{3}{2}$ $-\dfrac{1}{5}$ $-\dfrac{3}{4}$ $-\dfrac{2}{5}$ $-\dfrac{2}{5}$ -4 -1

Name_____

How Big Is The Pool?

Solve the pool problems to finish the pool puzzle. Follow the clues to find the places to write solutions into the puzzle. Each clue gives the dimensions and/or the capacity (volume) of a pool. In each case, one dimension is missing. Find the missing dimensions. (V = volume, d = depth, w = width, l = length.) All measurements are in feet, except V which is cubic feet.)

Across

1. V = 12,000; l = 40; w = 25   d = _____

2. l = 87; w = 6; d = 4   V = _____

4. d = 2; l = 163; w = 20   V _____

5. V = 1500; d = 15; w = 10   l = _____

6. w = 25; d = 9; V = 15,750   l = _____

7. V = 4840; l = 22; w = 11   d = _____

8. d = 8; V = 9040; l = 10   w = _____

9. V = 16,000; w = 10; l = 100   d = _____

10. d = 8; w = 2; l = 13   V = _____

11. w = 20; V = 16,000; d = 5   l = _____

14. d = 3; w = 3; l = 89   V = _____

16. w = 8; d = 5; l = 15   V = _____

Down

1. d = 10; l = 60; w = 31   V = _____

3. w = 5; d = 4; l = 203   V = _____

5. V = 69,200; l = 200; d = 2   w = _____

7. w = 3; d = 1; l = 72   V = _____

9. l = 50; w = 10; V = 9000   d = _____

10. w = 50; d = 8; V = 80,000   l = _____

12. V = 3400; l = 10; d = 5   w = _____

13. w = 2; d = 6; V = 1320   l = _____

15. V = 2400; l = 15; w = 10   d = _____

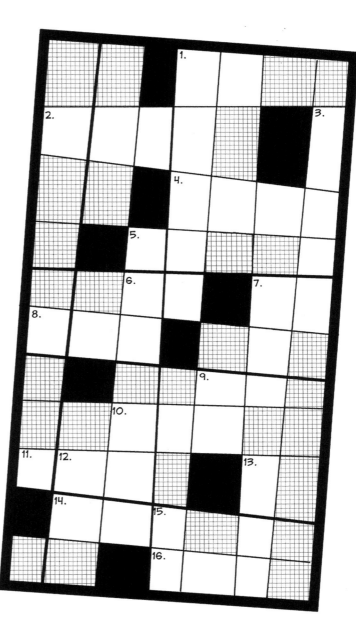

WHEN IS THE RIGHT TIME TO TALK TURKEY?

Any time is a good time to talk turkey, because there are a flock of interesting turkey facts to share. To find some of these facts and solve a turkey puzzle, start by evaluating the expressions. The puzzle is a bit tricky, but if you do it right, you'll get a semi-mathematical statement that tells you the best way to greet a turkey.

1. $8^2 + 6^2 - 25\%$ **of 12** Americans eat turkey on Thanksgiving.

2. $25^2 + 20\%$ **of 250** million pounds of turkey are eaten each Thanksgiving.

3. Wow! The weight of the heaviest domesticated turkey on record is
$11^2 - 7^2 + 33\frac{1}{3}\%$ **of 42** pounds.

4. The flying speed of wild turkeys can be as great as $5^2 + 6^2 - 75\%$ **of 8** miles per hour.

5. It takes about $12^2 - 8^2 + 213\%$ **of 0** pounds of feed to raise a 30-pound turkey.

6. Turkeys will have $30^2 + 50^2 + 10\%$ **of** 10^3 feathers at maturity.

7. It takes turkey eggs $7^2 - 6^2 + 50\%$ **of 30** days to hatch.

8. Turkeys live almost $1^2 + 2^2 + 3^2 - 400\%$ **of 1** years.

9. On a quiet day, gobbling turkeys can be heard
from $2 \cdot (\frac{1}{2})^2 + 2 \cdot (\frac{1}{2})^2$ mile(s) away.

KEY

Value	80	86	1	75	2	97	28	675	50	10	55	3500	1760	650	17
x	)	2	3	4	!	(	B	E	F	G	L	O	S	T	W

Puzzle

The numbers beneath the blanks are the problem numbers. After you evaluate each expression, find the value on the key and the letter or symbol connected to that value. Write this in the blank.

___ ___ ___ ___ ↑ ___ ___ ___ ↑
 1   8   6   7   3   4   2   5   9

Name_____

WHAT'S THE RIDDLE IN THE MIDDLE?

Find the correct equation in the middle of each row, and these will lead you to the solution of a math riddle.

Somewhere in the middle of each row, there is an equation with a solution of (-3). Locate and shade the entire equation. (Equations will not extend to either end of a row.)

1	m	$\frac{1}{2}$n	=	12	+	(-n	+	-5n)	÷	2	=	9	+	b	(4)
2	8	(2)	=	k	=	-6	—	-3	=	2c	=	4	=	x	y
3	p	(4)	+	3	=	15	+	(3)	$\frac{1}{3}$d	+	d	=	-4	+	f
4	(12)	i³	—	i	+	24	=	0	—	10i	+	r	=	(5)	r
5	q²	÷	4	=	-2	=	a²	(6)	÷	27	=	2	+	m	(4)
6	-s	+	3t	+	t	+	7	=	t	—	2	÷	g	=	7
7	(7)	2w	4	+	6	=	(5e²	—	e)	÷	8	=	$\frac{2}{8}$	+	$\frac{1}{8}$
8	√16	+	i³	=	-15	—	i	=	-6	—	6	+	v	=	9

Identify the circled letters that fall within equations. Unscramble these letters to solve the riddle.

Puzzle

When a poor math student was asked how he managed to avoid failing algebra, he replied,

" __ __ __ __ __ , __

__ __ __ __ __ __ __ . "

Name_____

WHAT'S THE MARK OF A GOOD SLUG RACE?

Yes, slugs do race! Slug racing is a popular sport, particularly in the rainy northwestern United States, where slugs are plentiful.

"Race" these slugs by drawing a path for each slug through the numbers or expressions of the same value. (Make sure the path connects the stars by these expressions.) Use a different color to draw each path. Every path will pass through some letters. The sticky slugs will pick up these letters and drop them in the boxes at the ends of their paths.

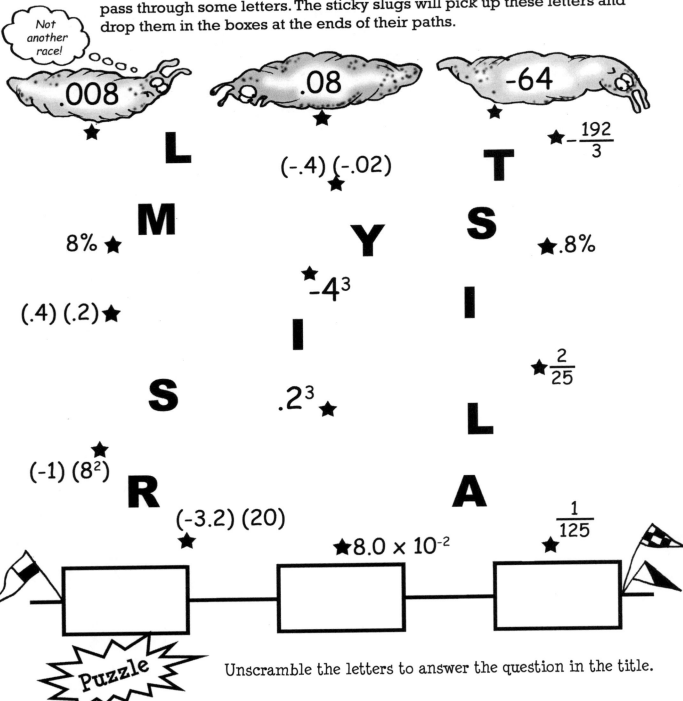

Not another race!

.008

.08

-64

$-\dfrac{192}{3}$

L

M

$(-.4)\,(-.02)$

T

S

8%

Y

.8%

-4^3

(.4) (.2)

I

I

S

$.2^3$

$\dfrac{2}{25}$

L

$(-1)\,(8^2)$

R

A

$(-3.2)\,(20)$

$\dfrac{1}{125}$

$\bigstar 8.0 \times 10^{-2}$

Unscramble the letters to answer the question in the title.

Name

WILL YOU TAKE IT OR LEAVE IT?

The answers are there. Some are wrong, some are right.

Each top block (shaded) contains an expression. The two white blocks beneath have choices for factoring. Decide whether the factoring in a white box is correct. Then write TAKE or LEAVE on that block. Take the letters from the correct answer boxes and leave the others behind.

1. $8y + 12$

T $(3y)(4+8)$

$(2y+3)(4)$ G

PUZZLE

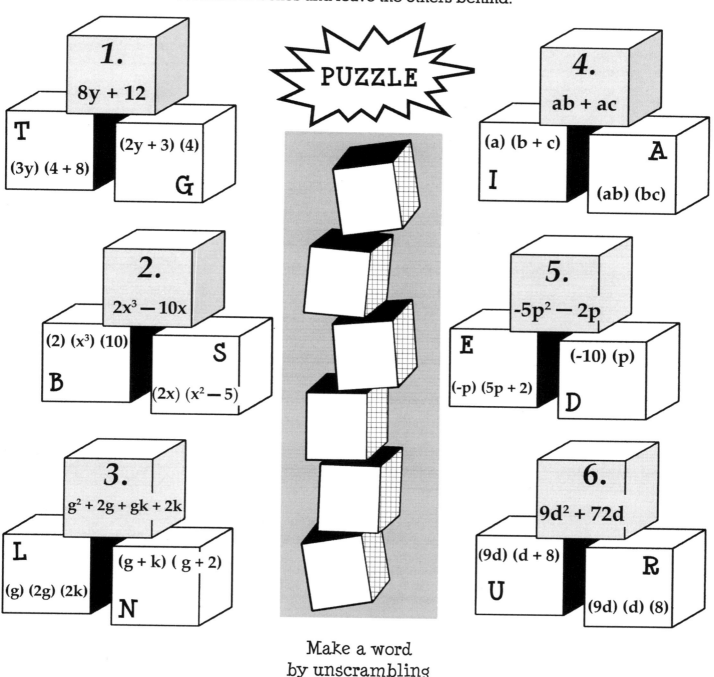

4. $ab + ac$

(a) $(b+c)$ I

A $(ab)(bc)$

2. $2x^3 - 10x$

$(2)(x^3)(10)$ B

S $(2x)(x^2-5)$

5. $-5p^2 - 2p$

E $(-p)(5p+2)$

$(-10)(p)$ D

3. $g^2 + 2g + gk + 2k$

L $(g)(2g)(2k)$ N

$(g+k)(g+2)$

6. $9d^2 + 72d$

$(9d)(d+8)$ U

R $(9d)(d)(8)$

Make a word by unscrambling the letters from the correct white boxes.

Name_____

WHAT'S THE DISTRACTION?

Are you ever distracted from your homework? Maybe not, but many math students are. Show your skill at graphing inequalities, and solve the puzzle to learn about math distractions at the same time.

1.

ON THE NEXT PAGE, PAGE 55, YOU WILL FIND TWELVE SMALL GRIDS FOR GRAPHING. GRAPH EACH OF THE SETS OF INEQUALITIES ON THE GRID WITH THE CORRESPONDING NUMBER. SHOW THE INEQUALITY BY SHADING THE AREA OF THE GRID COVERED BY THE SOLUTION OF THE SET.

HEY!

I can't concentrate with all these distractions.

ding dong

crash!

Sets of Inequalities

1. $x \leq -2$
   $y \geq 2$

2. $y \leq \frac{4}{3}x - 2$
   $y \leq -\frac{3}{4}x + 3$

3. $x \geq 0$
   $x + y \geq 5$

4. $x + y < 2$
   $x + y > -2$

5. $y > x$
   $y < -x$

6. $y \geq x$
   $x + y \leq 4$

7. $y < -x$
   $x + y < 3$

8. $y \geq 2x - 1$
   $y \leq -x + 1$

9. $y \geq 2$
   $y \geq 2x - 1$

10. $x + y < 4$
    $x - y > 4$

11. $x - 2 \leq y$
    $x + 2 \geq y$

2.

When you are finished with the graphing, notice the letters that fall within the shaded areas. Write these letters in the blanks above the matching problem (grid) number.

Common homework distractions are

Puzzle

$\overline{}_{9}$ $\overline{}_{5}$ $\overline{}_{6}$ $\overline{}_{6}$ $\overline{}_{10}$,

$\overline{}_{2}$ $\overline{}_{1}$ $\overline{}_{11}$ $\overline{}_{10}$,

& $\overline{}_{8}$ $\overline{}_{4}$ $\overline{}_{3}$ $\overline{}_{2}$ $\overline{}_{10}$

Use with page 55.

Name _____

Puzzle 48

Graph each set of inequalities (from page 54) on the grid with the corresponding number.

Notice the letters that fall within your shaded areas. Use these to fill in the puzzle blanks on page 54.

1

V   Q

S   R

2

M

Q   N

P   D

3

H   O

E

G   F

4

R

U

T

P

5

R   I

O

E

U

W   Y

6

O

L   P

M

7

C   F

D   E

8

J

G

I

H

9

C   S

Q   P

10

D

C

B

S

11

V

R

U

D   T

Use with page 54.

Name_____

DO YOU KNOW THESE RABBIT FACTS?

Puzzle 49

Find some "hare"-raising facts about rabbits by practicing your equation-solving skills. Solve each equation for **n**. Use the ordered pairs given for each example. Your solution will give a number that answers a rabbit question.

When you are finished answering the questions, stay on the rabbit track by completing the graph on the next page.

*Write the value of **n** on the line before the problem.*

_____ 1. How many bunny rabbits can a mother rabbit have in a year? (12, 9)
$x + 3y = n - 1$

_____ 2. How high (in inches) can a rabbit jump? (17, 11)
$(x - y)^2 = n$

_____ 3. What is the range (in degrees) of a rabbit's field of view? (11, 15)
$30x + 2y = n$

_____ 4. In miles per hour, how fast can rabbits run? (9, 12)
$x + 2y = n - 2$

_____ 5. How many different breeds of rabbits have been discovered? (5, 8)
$2x + 5y = n$

_____ 6. How many teeth do rabbits have? (6.5, 11.5)
$x + y + 10 = n$

_____ 7. How many million chocolate Easter bunnies are produced each year? (9, 3)
$9x + 3y = n$

_____ 8. What percent of adults prefer mild chocolate to dark chocolate bunnies? (9, 6)
$5x + 4y = n + 4$

_____ 9. What percent of adults believe that you should eat the ears of a chocolate bunny first? (7, 6)
$10x + y = n$

_____10. What percent of adults believe that you should eat the tail of a chocolate bunny first? (7, 3)
$x - n = y$

Use with page 57.

Name_____

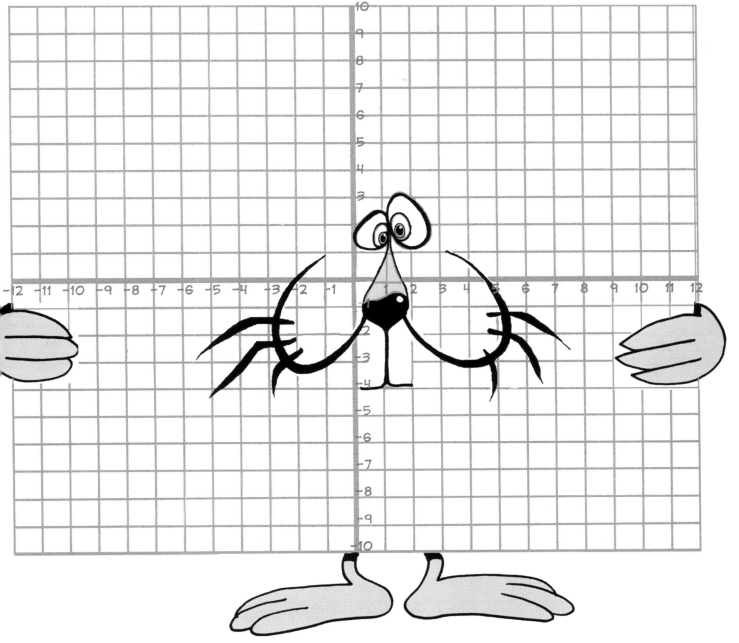

Plot the points in each group. Connect the points for each group in order.

A. (0,–2) (0,–4) (2,–4) (2,–2)

B. (3,1) (4,3) (3,4) (4,7) (10,3) (4,10) (1,4) $(-\frac{1}{2},3\frac{1}{2})$ (–5,8)
   (–9,1) (–5,5) (–2,3) (–2,2) (–1,1)

C. CREATE A BODY FOR THE RABBIT BY PLOTTING YOUR OWN POINTS!
   WRITE YOUR POINTS ON THE LINE:

_____

Use with page 56.

Name_____

ISN'T SOMETHING MISSING?

Max finished his homework (and he solved everything correctly), but didn't take very good care of it afterwards. He crumpled it up in his backpack. Now it is all torn up and full of holes. Help him figure out what is missing, so that he can fix it up. Select the missing values from the numbers in the key.

MATH HOMEWORK

Solve for x.

MATH HOMEWORK	MAX'S ANSWERS
1. $2x$ ▨ $+ 5x - 7 = 11$	$x = 2$
2. $-3x - 5 +$ ▨ $- 7 = -6$	$x = 7$
3. $8 - 4x + 9x$ ▨ $= -19$	$x = -4$
4. -16 ▨ $-7 + 8x = -17$	$x = \frac{1}{2}$
5. $2x - 5 - 6x$ ▨ $= 20$	$x = -9$
6. ▨ $- 7x - 3 = -27$	$x = 4$
7. $5 = 7x - 2(x +$ ▨ $) = 4$	$x = \frac{1}{5}$
8. $14 +$ ▨ $+ 5x - 8 = -27$	$x = -3$
9. $7x$ ▨ $3 + 2x - 7 = -7$	$x = \frac{1}{3}$

Key

-11	I
-7	L
6x	E
7x	F
7	T
+ 4x	H
-6x	C
+	Y
12	A
-	N
1	O
$\frac{1}{3}$	R
+4	S
÷	C
4	G

 Puzzle

The numbers beneath the blank lines are the problem numbers. Find the missing piece from that problem on the key. Write the matching letter in the blank to finish the simile:

Solving equations is like

___ ___ ___ ___ ___ ___ ___ ___ ___ ___ ___ ___ ___ ___ .
2   5   3   3   5   9   6   5   9   4   7   3   8   1

Name_____

Answer Key

Puzzle 1 (pg 7)

1. 37
2. 3.3
3. 50
4. 5
5. 300
6. 3
7. 70
8. 7
9. 250
10. 60
11. 36
12. 46

Riddle Answer: Left: D TST S NW;
Right: UGTBK (Bonus: *Sam*: The test is
now. *Pam*: You've got to be kidding!)

Puzzle 2 (pg 8)

Answers:
1. That is.
2. Time flies.
3. to the point of making one sick
4. Let the buyer beware.
5. You must have the body.
6. other self

Puzzle 3 (pg 9)

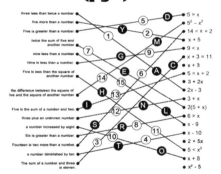

Matched answers, from top to bottom:

A-1: $2x - 3$;   Y-2: $x + 5$;
D-5: $5 > x$;   E-7: $2(5 + x)$;
L-15: $9 - x$;   G-9: $9 < x$;
H-11: $5 < x^2$;   M-14: $5^2 - x^2$;
I-13: $5 = x + 2$;   O-10: $x + 8$;
R-8: $6 > x$;   S-6: $14 = 2 + x$;
T-4: $x - 10$;   C-3: $x + 3 = 11$
N-12: $3 + x$

Riddle Answer: *You'll need* AN
ENGLISH-TO-MATH DICTIONARY!

Puzzle 4 (pg 10)

Recipe Answer: $1\frac{1}{2}$ C butter, $2\frac{1}{2}$ C sugar;
9 eggs; 8 oz chocolate; 1 C flour; $4\frac{1}{2}$ t
vanilla; 4 tsp baking powder, $1\frac{1}{8}$ tsp salt

Items at bottom: a. 45; b. $12\,\pi$; c. $36\,\pi$;
d. 28.26 in^3

Puzzle 5 (pg 11)

Flag measurements:
1. A = 10m; S = 24m^2;
2. N = $\sqrt{85m}$; T = 21m^2; 3. W = 13m;
R = 30m; 4. G = 12m; I = 36m;
5. O = 17m; H = 60m^2; 6. L = 20m;
E = 60m.

Riddle Answer: The Pythagorean
Theorem works for right triangles.
It does not work for wrong triangles.

Puzzle 6 (pg 12)

Riddle Answer: when it's a fraction.
Equation answers, in order of the letters
in the riddle:

W = $\frac{11}{10}$;   H = $\frac{1}{2}$;   E = $\frac{3}{5}$;   N = $\frac{1}{10}$;

I = $\frac{6}{5}$;   T = $\frac{1}{4}$;   S = $\frac{2}{5}$;   A = $\frac{1}{5}$;

F = $\frac{3}{4}$;   R = $\frac{1}{8}$;   A = $\frac{3}{8}$;   C = $\frac{7}{10}$;

T = $\frac{1}{25}$;   I = $\frac{3}{10}$;   O = $\frac{13}{10}$;   N = $\frac{4}{5}$

Puzzle 7 (pg 13)

1. 24
2. 99
3. 26
4. 33
5. 30
6. 29
7. 21
8. 44
9. 34
10. 35
11. 31
12. 28

Bonus Answer: Hawaiian

Puzzle 8 (pg 14)

2 Across is the clue for 16 Down.
8 Across is correct as is.
9 Across is correct as is.
11 Across is the clue for 20 Across.
13 Across is the clue for 7 Down.
14 Across is correct as is.
15 Across is the clue for 10 Down.
17 Across is correct as is.
18 Across is the clue for 3 Down.
19 Across is correct as is.
20 Across is the clue for 11 Across
1 Down is correct as is.
3 Down is the clue for 15 Across.
4 Down is the clue for 5 Down.
5 Down is the clue for 12 Down.
7 Down is the clue for 13 Across
10 Down is the clue for 18 Across.
12 Down is the clue for 4 Down.
16 Down is the clue for 2 Across.

Puzzle 9 (pg 15)

Riddle Answer: Starbucks

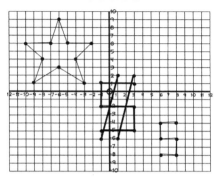

Puzzle 10 (pg 16)

1. $x + (x + 2) = 74$
(x = 36; numbers are 36 and 38)
2. $x + (x + 3) + (x + 6) = 42$
(x = 11; numbers are 11, 14, 17)
3. $x + (x + 4) + (x + 8) + (x + 12) = 56$
(x = 8; numbers are 8, 12, 16, 20)
4. $x + (x + 3) + (x + 6) = 63$
(x = 18; numbers are 18, 21, 24)

Riddle Answer: in a row

Puzzle 11 (pg 17)

1. $24\frac{1}{2}$ ft; J= Lee Redmond
2. 60 lb; G = Michel Lotito
3. 8; I = Jackie Bibby
4. 17.5 ft; B = Hans Langseth
5. $75\frac{2}{3}$ hrs; F = Arulanantham Suresh
Joachim
6. 66; C = Joey Chestnut
7. 1500; H = Elaine Davidson
8. 88; A = Ashrita Furman
9. 18; E = Francisco Peinado Toledo
10. 94; D = Kim Seung Do

Puzzle 12 (pg 18)

1. 1 (A)
2. 280 (U)
3. 28 (Y)
4. 39 (D)
5. 19 (E)
6. 110 (H)
7. 26 (L)
8. 98 (G)
9. 21 (L)
10. 41 (O)
11. 250 (N)
12. 5 (J)
13. 59 (U)

14. 698 (T)
The figure is: a jelly doughnut

Puzzle 13 (pg 19)

Red = squares k and t; Blue = squares a and o; Green squares q and x; Orange = squares g and p; Yellow: squares f and l; Pink: squares c and j; Purple: b and s; Brown: squares v and w

Puzzle 14 (pg 20)

1. Joe = 112
2. Juan = 135
3. Jeremy = 225
4. Joel = 125
5. Jamal = 156
6. Jude = 180
7. Jason

Diameter of wrestling circle = 9 m.
Area of wrestling circle = 63.585 m.

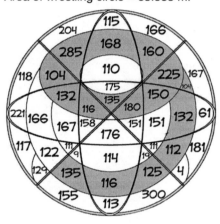

Puzzle 15 (pg 21)

1. 245 ft
2. 456 ft
3. 420 ft
4. $3\frac{1}{2}$ min
5. $4\frac{1}{2}$ ft
6. 61°

Tallest coaster is *Kingda Ka*.

Puzzle 16 (pg 22)

1. O
2. R
3. N
4. B
5. E
6. U
7. M
8. R
9. Y
10. U

Answer: I've got your number.

Puzzle 17 (pg 23)

1. 1 hr
2. 60 mph
3. 288 min
4. 10 hr
5. 62 mph
6. yes
7. no

Riddle: Sixty is nifty.

Puzzle 18 (pg 24)

Knight 7:
  Draw a path to the hut ($2\sqrt{196}$) to the castle (7^3) to the log (77) to the fish (420) to the frog ($11^2 + 5$) to the unicorn ($2^6 - 1$).

Knight 3:
  Draw a path to the troll ($3^2 + 15$) to the boot (918) to the bird in the tree (525) to the rock with the devil behind ($2^5 + 1$) to the fish (420) to the bare tree (972) to the frog ($11^2 + 5$) to the rock ($\sqrt{144}$) to the witch's hat (369).

Knight 4:
  Draw a path to the bearded character (800) to the mushroom ($\sqrt{64}$) to the troll ($3^2 + 15$) to the dragon (256) to the snake (4) to the rock ($\sqrt{144}$) to the fish (420) to the bare tree (972) to the flower (44).

Knight 5:
  Draw a path to the bearded character (800) to the bird in the tree (525) to the bottom of the tree ($-5 + \sqrt{10,000}$) to the fish (420) to the fairy (275) to the fish ($\sqrt{625}$) to the tree with the hole ($2^4 + 2^3 + 1$).

1. No, there is one winner. Knight 5 is the only knight to go through seven obstacles.
2. The object that holds a multiple of all numbers is the fish (420).

Puzzle 19 (pg 25)

Player	Hits	Digs	Assists	Aces	Blocks
Sarah	1	0	10	4	1
Susan	0	2	3	4	7
Sierra	8	3	3	0	2
Samantha	2	0	3	4	3
Stacey	0	3	5	4	0
Stephanie	2	6	1	4	7
Sasha	8	0	1	4	7
Cecilia	3	2	6	4	1

1. 4
2. Missing Stats:
Susan—Digs $\sqrt[5]{32}$ or 2;
Stephanie—Blocks $6^2 - 29$ or 7; $\sqrt[3]{27}$ or 3
Cecilia—Hits $\sqrt[3]{27}$ or 3; $6^2 - 29$
(The answers for Stephanie and Cecilia are interchangeable, but each answer should be used only one time.)

Puzzle 20 (pg 26)

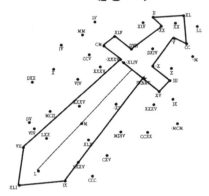

Connect the answers in this order.
1. LXXV
2. XLI
3. VII
4. −XXXV
5. CM
6. XLV
7. DVII
8. −XX
9. II
10. XL
11. CC
12. V
13. CCCXC
14. III
15. XV
16. −XLIV

Date 3/15/−44 (March 15, 44 BC). Julius Caesar was killed with a dagger on this date (known as the Ides of March).

Puzzle 21 (pg 27)

1. $60

2. $8
3. $33
4. $99
5. $49
6. $4
7. $928
8. $9
9. $1290
10. $654
11. $21
12. $50
13. $5
14. $654
15. $24

Answer grid spells "49ers."

1	2	6	$	2	8	7	4	9	4	9	2	6	4	$	1	$	2	3	$	2
4	$	3	$	3	$	0	$	$	$	$	2	$	7	8	5	4	$	4	$	3	6
7	6	5	1	6	6	2	9	2	$	3	$	3	7	9	$	2	2	7	1	8
2	0	5	2	5	5	5	2	7	7	5	2	6	6	6	3	8	9	$	2	6
8	$	9	9	6	4	$	8	6	$	3	3	$	$	4	9	6	$	0	0	5
9	2	5	0	$	3	2	$	3	0	1	4	2	9	5	$	$	0	4	$	5
4	6	3	$	3	8	5	7	8	$	0	5	6	$	2	4	$	2	0	5	6
6	1	9	5	2	$	3	6	6	2	5	8	8	4	0	$	$	1	5	0	9
$	$	3	0	2	3	4	5	3	1	$	5	4	0	9	0	2	0	0	6	$
3	$	7	5	1	$	3	9	6	6	5	9	7	$	2	6	1	$	6	1	2

Puzzle 22 (pg 28)

A $x > -6$
B $x \le 1$
C $x \ge -14$
D $x < -10$
E $x > 4$
F $x \le -11$
G $x < -6$
H $x \ge -\frac{1}{5}$

Sam's trail goes from A to C to B to D to F to G to H to E to the ambulance.

Puzzle 23 (pg 29)

1. $t = \frac{1}{2}$
2. $m = 2\frac{1}{3}$
3. $a = 100$
4. $e = 1.5$
5. $n = 166$
6. $s = 300$
7. $h = \frac{3}{4}$
8. $t = 8$
9. $i = 38$
10. $m = .01$
11. $i = 20$
12. $a = .1$
13. $c = 30$
14. $a = 6$

Puzzle Answer: mathematicians

Puzzle 24 (pg 30)

1. 1
2. $3\frac{1}{2}$
3. -2
4. 0
5. 40

6. 10
7. -4
8. 45
9. $\frac{1}{8}$
10. 17
11. 400
12. -19

Conversation: Hey, that was . . . not the substitution I had in mind.

Puzzle 25 (pg 31)

1–5. $n + 6c < 4g$
5–11. $4g = 80 - 5a^2 + (-5v)$
11–15. $-5v - 90 = -o^2$
15–19. $o^2 + 70 = 3t$
19–25. $3t \div 10d = e + 20$
23–29. $e + 20 > 2s - 9r$

Snail to waiter: Don't serve escargot!

Puzzle 26 (pg 32)

1. $\frac{3}{12}$ or $\frac{1}{4}$
2. $\frac{4}{12}$ or $\frac{1}{3}$
3. $\frac{7}{60}$
4. $\frac{1}{560}$
5. $\frac{3}{14}$
6. $\frac{3}{70}$
7. $\frac{6}{35}$
8. 3

In the drawer, there will be 3 red socks, 2 purple socks, 3 green socks, 1 yellow sock. The rest (7) will be white.
BONUS: $\frac{7}{15}$

Puzzle 27 (pg 33)

1. 318
2. 95
3. 8133
4. 263
5. 81
6. 3500
7. 259
8. 81
9. 6708
10. 249
11. 78
12. 3782

Puzzle Solution:
It's got its ups and downs!

Puzzle 28 (pg 34)

1. 25.12 in^2
2. 540°
3. 33 min
4. 50.24 in
5. 180°
6. 3:30

7. 60°
8. 125.6 in^2
9. 12:10
10. 420°
11. 188.4 in
12. 8:50
13. 8:45
14. 195°

Riddle Answer: lunch time

Puzzle 29 (pg 35)

1. $x = 50$ (h)
2. $x = 1$ (s)
3. $x = -45$ (o)
4. $x = -17$ (e)
5. $x = -1$ (f)
6. $x = 8$ (l)
7. $x = 75$ (d)
8. $x = 7$ (t)
9. $x = -55$ (a)
10. $x = -110$ (i)
11. $x = 80$ (n)
12. $x = 10$ (b)

The suspect is: The Salsa Bandito.

Puzzle 30 (pg 36)

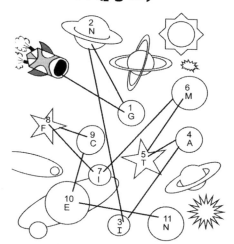

1. 1.43×10^5 (g)
2. 1.43×10^7 (n)
3. 1.43×10^2 (i)
4. 1.43×10^{-3} (a)
5. 1.43×10^{-1} (t)
6. 1.43×10^6 (m)
7. 1.43×10^0 (i)
8. 1.43×10^3 (f)
9. 1.43×10^8 (c)
10. 1.43×10^{-2} (e)
11. 1.43×10^1 (n)

The mystery ship is *The Magnificent.*

Puzzle 31 (pg 37)

Clockwise from top right:
N – Shade 10 and 1 (1, 10)

X – no shading
I – Shade –2 and –2 (–2, –2)
E – Shade –14 and –5 (–5, –14)
U – Shade –6 and –3 (–3, –6)
R – Shade –1 and 2 (–1, 2)
C – no shading
O – Shade 0 and 6 (0, 6)
T – Shade –1.5 and 0 (–1.5, 0)
P – Shade 18 and 3 (3, 18)
A starburst might be caused by an *eruption*.

Puzzle 32 (pg 38)

Angle W = 25°
Angle H = 90°
Angle E = 61°
Angle N = 91°
Angle I = 38°
Angle T = 75°
Angle S = 125°
Angle O = 51°
Angle B = 155°
Angle U = 99°
Answer: when it's obtuse

Puzzle 33 (pg 39)

C = 15
F = –2
T = 9.91
P = –25
R = 5/6
Y = 16
A = –12
S = –20
O = –8
E = –3.2
D = 69
M = –1
Puzzle: matador's cape

Puzzle 34 (pg 40)

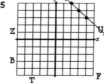

1. R   2. A
3. E   O   X
    X   O   E
4. O P 5. O S I T E S
    O   B
    N 6. T A N G E N T
    E   U
    N 7. S Q U A 8. R E
    T   E   A
                          9. T E R M S
            10. P I
                      O

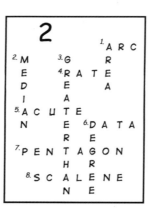

2
                    1. A R C
2. M   3. G   R
E   4. R A T E
D   E   A
I   A
5. A C U T E
N   E   6. D A T A
                R   E
7. P E N T A G O N
                H   R
        8. S C A L E N E
                N   E

Puzzle 35 (pg 41)

Tables of ordered pairs will vary.

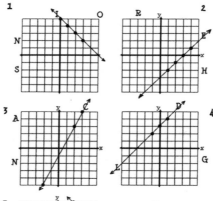

Geometry fan is Euclid

Puzzle 36 (pg 42)

D = 1588
E = 1914
G = 1812
H = 1532
I = 1066
N = 1517
O = 1095
R = 1704
S = 1643
T = 1519
Y = 1346
Bonus: to get history in order.

Puzzle 37 (pg 43)

1. (2, 6) Rattlesnake Canyon
2. (–4, –12) Lizard Races
3. (4, 7) Sparkling Oasis
4. (–3, 0) Cactus Juice Stand
5. (1, 5) Tumbleweed Café
6. (3, 9) Dreadful Sandstorm
7. (–6, –5) Dune Buggy Rental Shop
8. (–2, –1) Bone Dry Gulch

Puzzle 38 (pg 44)

n – 6
e – 36
d – 12
i – 63
k – 220
c – 93
r – 44
t – 60
Bonus: the under stick dance

Puzzle 39 (pg 45)

1. x = 9
2. x = 10
3. x = 2
4. x = 12
5. x = 0
6. x = 4
7. x = 6
8. x = 25
9. x = 8
10. x = 11
Puzzle: Just the fax, ma'am.
Bonus: safe combination: 0–25–8–4–10

Puzzle 40 (pg 46)

A = $-1\frac{1}{2}$ M = –1
B = 27   N = 1
C = $\frac{1}{4}$ O = 0
E = $\frac{1}{16}$ R = –9
F = $-\frac{1}{8}$ S = 3
G = –8   T = 9
H = 4   U = 2
I = –4   V = 6
K = 8   Y = $-\frac{1}{4}$

Puzzle Answer:
Try not to get too negative about math.

Puzzle 41 (pg 47)

1. A = 11; B = 5; C = 2; D = 4; E = $70
2. G = 6; H = 7; I = 3; K = 10
3. L = 60; N = 40; Q = 104; R = 62
4. S = 28; T = 30; U = 32
Puzzle: quick change artists

Puzzle 42 (pg 48)

1. 2
2. $-\frac{2}{5}$
3. -3
4. 1
5. -4
6. $-\frac{1}{5}$
7. 0
8. -1
9. $\frac{2}{3}$
10. $-\frac{3}{4}$
11. $-\frac{3}{2}$
12. $-\frac{1}{2}$

Circle: Skateboarder's path goes through 2, 3, 5, 6, 8, 10, 11, 12
Puzzle: rise over run

Puzzle 43 (pg 49)

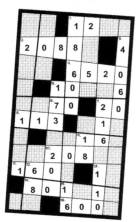

Across
1. d = 12
2. V = 2088
4. V = 6520
5. l = 10
6. l =70
7. d =20
8. w =113
9. d =16
10. V =208
11. l = 160
14. V = 801
16. V = 600

Down
1. V = 18,600
3. V = 4060
5. w = 173
7. V = 216
9. d = 18
10. l = 200
12. w = 68
13. l = 110
15. d = 16

Puzzle 44 (pg 50)

1. 97 = (
2. 675 = E
3. 86 =(2)
4. 55 = L
5. 80 =)
6. 3500 = O
7. 28 = B
8. 10 = G
9. 1 = B

Puzzle: $(GOB^2LE)^3$ (gobble, gobble, gobble)

Puzzle 45 (pg 51)

1. $-n + -5n \div 2 = 9$
2. $k = -6 - (-3)$
3. $\frac{1}{3}d + d = -4$
4. $i^3 - i + 24 = 0$
5. $a^2(6) \div 27 = 2$
6. $3t + t + 7 = t - 2$
7. $6 = 5e^2 - e \div 8$
8. $-15 - i = -6 - 6$

Circled letters within equations are n, k, d, d, i, i, a, t, t, t, e, i
Riddle answer: I didn't take it.

Puzzle 46 (pg 52)

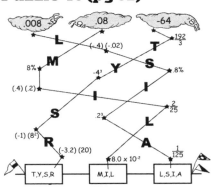

First Slug: from .008 to $(-.4)$ $(-.02)$ to .8% to $.2^3$ to $\frac{1}{125}$;
Picks up letters L, S, I, A

Second Slug: .08 to 8% to $(.4)$ $(.2)$ to $\frac{2}{25}$ to 8.0×10^{-2};
Picks up letters M, I, L

Third Slug: -64 to $\frac{192}{3}$ to -4^3 to (-1) (8^2) to (-3.2) (20);
Picks up letters T, Y, S, R

Puzzle: slimy trails

Puzzle 47 (pg 53)

1. G: $(2y + 3)(4)$
2. S: $(2x)(x^2 - 5)$
3. N: $(g + k)(g + 2)$
4. I: $(a)(b + c)$
5. E: $(-p)(5p + 2)$
6. U: $(9d)(d + 8)$
The word is: genius

Puzzle 48 (pgs 54–55)

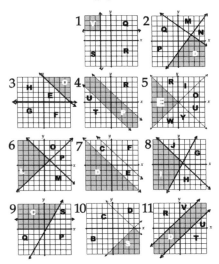

Puzzle answer: CELLS, DVDS, & IPODS

Puzzle 49 (pgs 56–57)

1. n = 40
2. n = 36
3. n = 360
4. n = 35
5. n = 50
6. n = 28
7. n = 90
8. n = 65
9. n = 76
10. n = 4

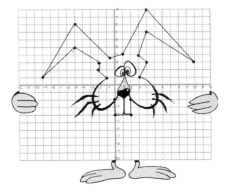

Puzzle 50 (pg 58)

What's covered up in each equation:
1. +4
2. 7x
3. −7
4. + 4x
5. −11
6. 4
7. 1
8. 6x
9. −

Solution: Solving equations is like filling in holes.